· All Around the ·
Neighborhood

Explore Your World & Learn About People at Work Through Literacy-Rich Lessons,

10 Mini-Books, **7** File Folder Games, **60+** Reproducible Patterns,

80+ Literature Links, and a Wealth of Fun Activities

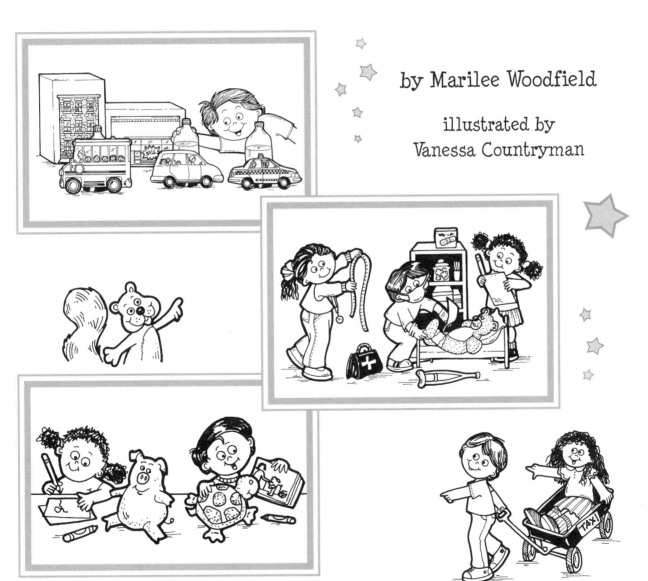

by Marilee Woodfield

illustrated by
Vanessa Countryman

Publisher
Key Education Publishing Company, LLC
Minneapolis, Minnesota

www.keyeducationpublishing.com

CONGRATULATIONS ON YOUR PURCHASE OF A KEY EDUCATION PRODUCT!

The editors at Key Education are former teachers who bring experience, enthusiasm, and quality to each and every product. Thousands of teachers have looked to the staff at Key Education for new and innovative resources to make their work more enjoyable and rewarding. We are committed to developing educational materials that will assist teachers in building a strong and developmentally appropriate curriculum for children.

PLAN FOR GREAT TEACHING EXPERIENCES WHEN YOU USE EDUCATIONAL MATERIALS FROM KEY EDUCATION PUBLISHING COMPANY, LLC

About the Author

Marilee Woodfield has graduated with a bachelor of science in human development from Brigham Young University. In addition to teaching and directing preschools for 20 years, she is the author of more than 15 resource books for early childhood educators, including Key Education's *Early Learning Center Games, Math Experiences for Young Learners, Do and Discover Science, Writing Experiences for Young Learners, Children Around the World: The Ultimate Class Field Trip,* and *All Around the Neighborhood.* Marilee also spends her time driving the family taxi service and completing various home-improvement projects. She currently resides in Texas with her husband and four children.

Credits

Author: Marilee Woodfield
Publisher: Sherrill B. Flora
Illustrator: Vanessa Countryman
Editors: Debra Olson Pressnall and Karen Seberg
Cover Design and Production:
    Annette Hollister-Papp
Page Design: Key Education Staff
Cover Photo Credits: © Comstock and
                  © Rubberball

Key Education welcomes manuscripts
and product ideas from teachers.
For a copy of our submission guidelines,
please send a self-addressed, stamped envelope to:

**Key Education Publishing Company, LLC
Acquisitions Department
9601 Newton Avenue South
Minneapolis, Minnesota 55431**

Copyright Notice

Standard Book Number: 978-1-602680-36-4
All Around the Neighborhood
Copyright © 2009 by Key Education Publishing Company, LLC
Minneapolis, Minnesota 55431

Table of Contents

Introduction

A neighborhood is made up of people who live and/or work together. If you were to look up the word *neighborhood* in the dictionary, you would find it defined as a place or people living near one another. Another similar word is *community*, which suggests thoughts of common interests and sharing. *All Around the Neighborhood* blends these two similar ideas into one resource. Children are invited to explore community places that are located in their school's neighborhood as well as places that may not be nearby. For example, your class may decide to learn about the grocery store, doctor's office, fire station, and recycling center. They will get to know people who work in these places, such as a grocer, nurse, firefighter, and sanitation worker.

Whether your neighborhood is rural, urban, or suburban, and whether you are connected to several neighborhoods or just one, there is something for everyone to enjoy while learning about neighborhoods and the people who work and live there.

So, who are the people in your neighborhood? *All Around the Neighborhood* explores many different business and public service facilities with diverse cross-curricular activities, such as writing books for the library, counting teeth at the dentist's office, testing gravity and friction at the park, and building a road in the construction zone. Begin your investigation by finding out which featured places can be found in your school's neighborhood. Next, talk about where children live and how they are important members of the neighborhood, too. Finally, continue the lessons by sharing more in-depth information and exploring the featured places with your class.

You will also find in this resource book the following:
- **Community Connections**—Ideas for taking children on excursions and inviting visitors to the classroom
- **Resources**—Suggested book titles to read aloud during group time and other interesting information about each theme
- **Kindergarten Corner**—Ideas that expand children's knowledge and challenge their thinking skills

How to Use This Book

Whether you're partial to firefighters or school lunch ladies, *All Around the Neighborhood* is a great resource for learning about neighborhood communities. Before taking off on "walking field trips" with the class, decide which places you would like the children to learn more about. Make a large, simple map on colorful craft paper by following the directions provided on the next page. When it is time to introduce the lesson, ask children to gather around you and look at the prepared map. Then, "walk" with your fingertips from the school to the featured building. Talk about the new theme, such as learning about the fire station, to find out what children already know about the topic. Each of the featured topics offers read-aloud book titles to introduce new vocabulary words and information as well as many fun activities for children to complete. Suggestions are also provided for setting up the dramatic play center—an important tool to help children process what they have been learning about their immediate world.

In addition to the fun ideas in this book, you will want to use your community resources to bring the activities to life. Plan excursions, invite visitors, and borrow tools, uniforms, and equipment, if possible, from community workers who live in your neighborhood. How to use these resources effectively is discussed further on page 6. There is so much to discover about people and places in your neighborhood—be sure also to draw from the curiosity of your children as you plan your lessons!

General Suggestions

Making a Map for "Walking Field Trips"

To highlight various points of interest in the neighborhood, make a map to show the locations of these sites. Decide which places the children will learn about and then make copies of the buildings and places that are provided on pages 8–15. (You may wish to create a map that corresponds to your school's neighborhood and can be used for the activity on page 30.) Color the drawings as desired before cutting them out. Attach a large sheet of craft paper to a bulletin board. Draw lines to represent streets and label them. To finish the map of the neighborhood, glue or tape the buildings in place.

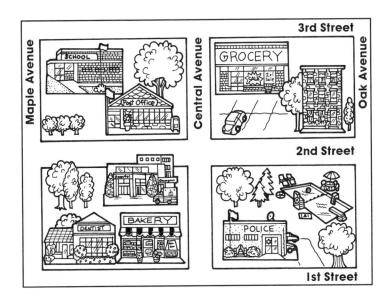

Creating Your Own Community

Children may enjoy making their own charming little neighborhood. To create this community, draw roads or streets with a broad-tipped marker on a large sheet of craft paper that has been taped to the floor. Stuff brown paper lunch bags with newspaper and staple the top edges together to close them. Copy the buildings on pages 10–15 and the vehicles provided in each thematic section onto card stock. Color the drawings as desired. Cut out and glue each building (e.g., library, post office, etc.) to a stuffed paper bag. To hold the vehicles upright, attach them to water bottles (see page 166). The children may be interested in drawing and coloring people on card stock to create a bustling neighborhood. If the paper people are cut out and attached to paper-towel cardboard tubes, they can be moved about the imaginary neighborhood. Invite children to arrange the buildings, people, and vehicles throughout the community. This special neighborhood wouldn't be complete without a name; children can use card stock to create a sign to welcome visitors to their imaginary community as well as construct trees, fire hydrants, and so on. This project will be ongoing for some time as children discover new things to add!

Inviting Workers into the Classroom

Before traveling to business and public service sites in the community, take advantage of resources right in your neighborhood. Poll the parents of children in your school to find out about their occupations. You will probably find a few who would be willing to talk about their insights and experiences. Here are some recommendations for organizing these events:

- **Plan ahead.** Give your visitors plenty of time to pencil you into their busy schedules. Check to see that all visitors meet your school's safety clearance procedures.

- **Ask visitors to show and tell.** Children will be more engaged during the presentation if your visitor brings a few interesting props (e.g., tools, uniform, protective boots and gloves, etc.) to show.

- **Give some guidelines.** Remind visitors that children have short attention spans. A 10-minute session is plenty of time for a presentation. Encourage your presenters to keep the talk on a level for young children and be interactive with them.

- **Send a note of appreciation.** Sending a card (or several) from children is a great way to show appreciation for a visitor's time and effort.

Meeting People at Work

When possible, use a digital camera to photograph people at work in the community for each unit of study. If an actual field trip can be arranged, take pictures of people and the tools they use when the children are present. Otherwise, if the site is farther away, try to arrange a time when you can visit the business or have a parent who works there take the photographs for you. Hang a piece of string or yarn across the classroom and use clothespins to display the pictures. During each theme, add the new photograph(s) to the collection to assemble a complete community of helpers "lined up" across the room.

Making the *Learning About My Neighborhood* Book ✳

Each neighborhood is different. Look around your school's neighborhood and help children understand the various jobs people do that impact your community. As your class learns about the different occupations featured in this resource book, use your photographs of actual people at work or copies of selected buildings and places provided on pages 8–15 and occupations on pages 17–27 to create a class book titled *Learning About My Neighborhood*. Gather large sheets of construction paper, sort the pictures by topic, and glue them accordingly on the paper. Write the name of the topic on each page with a black marker. You may also wish to glue a copy of the title page illustration provided below on construction paper. During group time, record what children have learned about a particular place and why those workers are important to your community. Each time the class learns about a new place in the neighborhood, make another page for your book. Once all of the "walking field trips" (real or imaginary) have been completed, collate the pages into a stack and punch holes along the left edge. Finish the book by lacing the pages together with yarn.

Learning About My Neighborhood

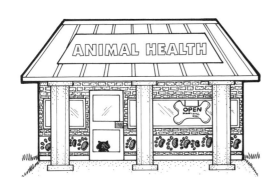

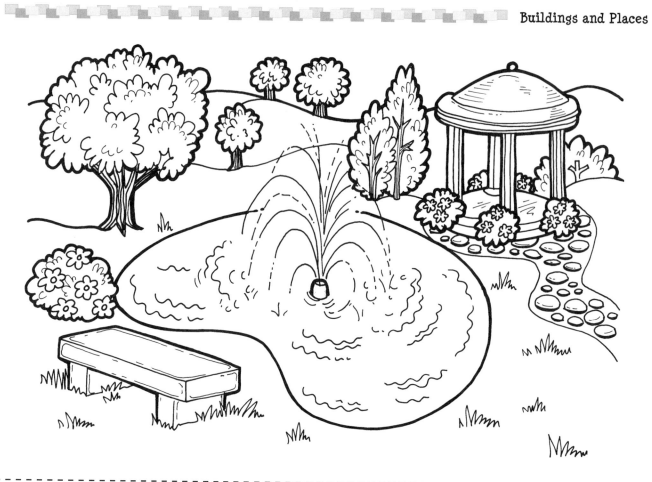

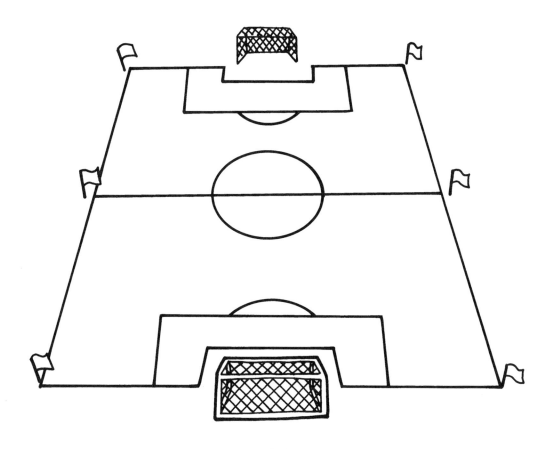

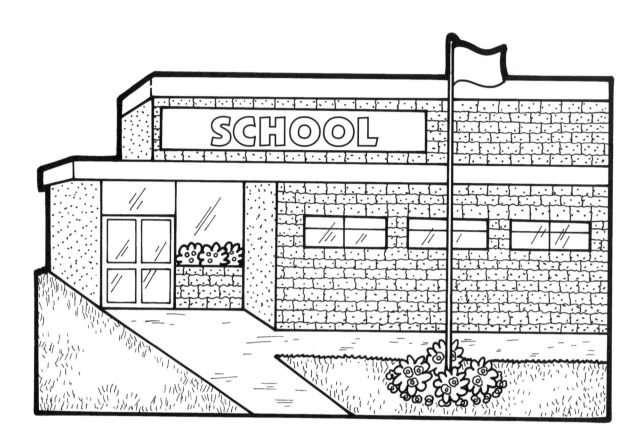

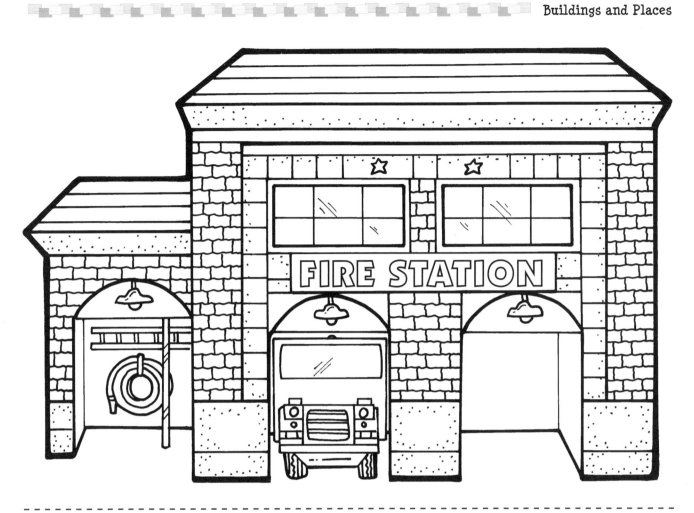

 All Around the Neighborhood

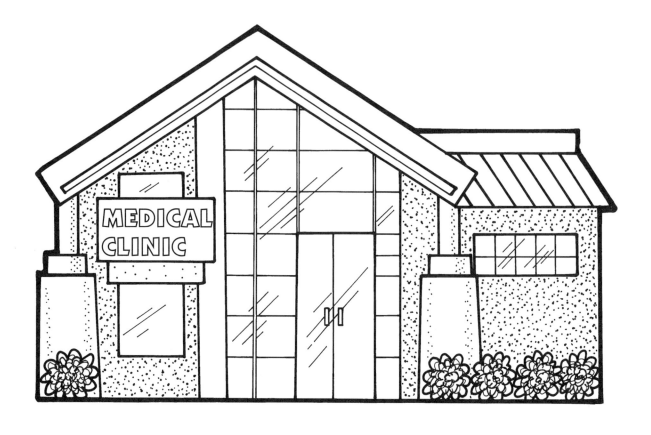

 All Around the Neighborhood

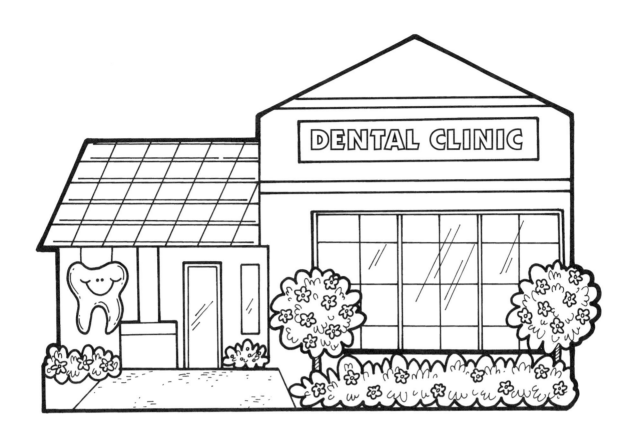

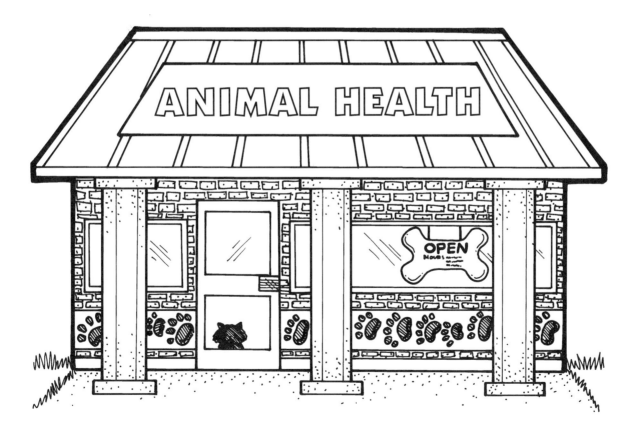

Making the *People at Work in the Neighborhood* Book

To help children recall what they have learned about various occupations, produce a class book that highlights the roles of community helpers and workers. If you have a digital camera, consider photographing people at work and making your own book with the photos. If it is not possible to take walking field trips to various businesses and community service buildings, determine which occupations you will focus on and make copies of the related pictures on pages 17–27 for your classroom books. The number of copies needed will vary depending on whether children will make individual booklets or collaborate on the project by each completing one of the pages for a class book. To assemble each book, use a copy of the cover page shown below or write the title on a sheet of construction paper. Collate the picture pages along with the title page and then bind the pages together by stapling them along the left edge. At the end of each theme, let children write an action word on the selected page to describe the kind of work the featured worker performs. For example, near the picture of the construction worker, a child may write the word *hammer* (*hamr*), *saw*, or *fixes*.

People at Work
in the Neighborhood

Park Worker

Lifeguard

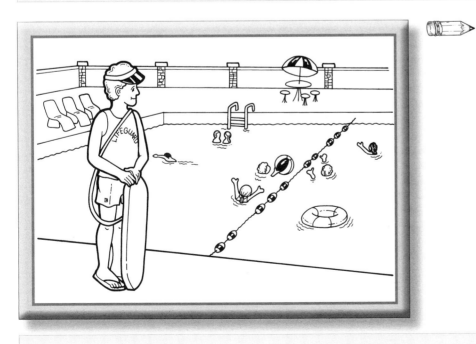

Coach

Construction Worker

Teacher

- -

Librarian

Firefighter

Police Officer

Doctor

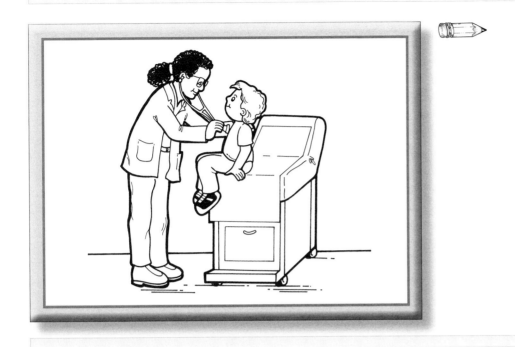

Nurse

Dentist

- -

Veterinarian

22

Mail Carrier

- -

Grocer

Baker

Chef

Carpenter

Plumber

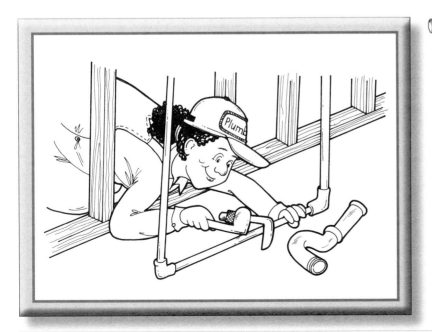

Bus Driver

- -

Driver/Operator

Florist

Janitor

Literature List

The following read-aloud titles are also provided in the thematic sections of this resource book.

My Neighborhood

The Best Town in the World by Byrd Baylor (Aladdin, 1986)

C Is for City by Nikki Grimes (Lothrop, Lee & Shepard, 1995)

The City ABC Book by Zoran Milich (Kids Can Press, 2002)

City Colors by Zoran Milich (Kids Can Press, 2006)

City 123 by Zoran Milich (Kids Can Press, 2007)

City Signs by Zoran Milich (Kids Can Press, 2002)

Community Helpers from A to Z by Bobbie Kalman (Crabtree Publishing Company, 1998)

Do Something in Your Community by Amanda Rondeau (ABDO, 2004)

Everybody Brings Noodles by Nora Dooley (Carolrhoda Books, 2005)

I Read Signs by Tana Hoban (Greenwillow, 1983)

The Mitten Tree by Candace Christiansen (Fulcrum, 1997)

Signs at School by Mary Hill (Children's Press, 2003)

Signs at the Airport by Mary Hill (Children's Press, 2003)

Signs at the Park by Mary Hill (Children's Press, 2003)

Signs on the Road by Mary Hill (Children's Press, 2003)

Signs at the Store by Mary Hill (Children's Press, 2003)

Sweet Dream Pie by Audrey Wood (Blue Sky Press, 1998)

Town Mouse, Country Mouse by Jan Brett (Putnam Juvenile, 1994)

Window by Jeannie Baker (Walker Books Ltd., 2002)

All About Me

A House for Hermit Crab by Eric Carle (Aladdin, 2005)

A House Is a House for Me by Mary Ann Hoberman, (Puffin, 2007)

Houses by Gallimard Jeunesse and Claude Delasfosse (Scholastic, 1998)

Houses and Homes by Ann Morris (HarperTrophy, 1995)

I Like Me by Nancy Carlson (Puffin, 1990)

Living in a Desert by Jan Kottke (Children's Press, 2000)

Living in a Rain Forest by Joanne Winne (Children's Press, 2000)

Living near a River by Joanne Winne (Children's Press, 2000)

Living on a Mountain by Joanne Winne (Children's Press, 2000)

Living on a Plain by Joanne Winne (Children's Press, 2000)

The Little House by Virginia Lee Burton (Houghton Mifflin, 1978)

My Home: Walls, Doors, Ceilings, and Floors by Lisa Bullard (Picture Window Books, 2003)

39 Uses for a Friend by Harriet Ziefert (G.P. Putnam's Sons 2001)

What I Do Best by Allia Zobel-Nolen (Reader's Digest, 2006)

What I Like About Me by Allia Zobel-Nolen (Reader's Digest, 2005)

My Home

A House for Hermit Crab by Eric Carle (Aladdin, 2005)

A House Is a House for Me by Mary Ann Hoberman (Puffin, 2007)

Houses by Gallimard Jeunesse and Claude Delasfosse (Scholastic, 1998)

Houses and Homes by Ann Morris (HarperTrophy, 1995)

Living in a Desert by Jan Kottke (Children's Press, 2000)

Living in a Rain Forest by Joanne Winne (Children's Press, 2000)

Living near a River by Joanne Winne (Children's Press, 2000)

Living on a Mountain by Joanne Winne (Children's Press, 2000)

Living on a Plain by Joanne Winne (Children's Press, 2000)

The Little House by Virginia Lee Burton (Houghton Mifflin, 1978)

My Home: Walls, Doors, Ceilings, and Floors by Lisa Bullard (Picture Window Books, 2003)

My Backyard

The Backyard by John Collier (Viking, 1993)

In My Backyard by Margriet Ruurs (Tundra, 2007)

The Snail's Spell by Joanne Ryder (Puffin, 1988)

The Park

Step-by-Step Tai Chi by Master Lam Kam Chuen (Fireside, 1994)

Window by Jeannie Baker (Greenwillow, 1991)

My School

Miss Nelson Is Missing! by Harry Allard (Houghton Mifflin, 1977)

Mrs. Toggle's Zipper by Robin Pulver (Aladdin, 1993)

School Days Around the World by Catherine Chambers (Dorling Kindersley Limited, 2007)

The Library

The Boy Who Was Raised by Librarians by Carla Morris Peachtree, 2007)

My Librarian Is a Camel: How Books Are Brought to Children Around the World by Margriet Ruurs (Boyds Mills Press, 2005)

Tomás and the Library Lady by Pat Mora (Knopf, 1997)

The Grocery Store

Do the Doors Open by Magic? And Other Supermarket Questions by Catherine Ripley (Owl Books, 1995)

Jake Baked the Cake by B.G. Hennessy (Puffin, 1992)

To Market, To Market by Anne Miranda (Voyager, 2001)

What's in Grandma's Grocery Bag? by Hui-Mei Pan (Star Bright Books, 2004)

Literature List (continued)

The Fire Station

Fire Fighter Piggy Wiggy by Christyan and Diane Fox (Handprint, 2001)

The Police Station

Aero and Officer Mike: Police Partners by Joan Plummer Russell (Boyds Mills Press, 2001)

Make Way for Ducklings by Robert McCloskey (Viking Press, 2001)

Never Talk to Strangers by Irma Joyce (Golden Books, 2009)

Officer Buckle and Gloria by Peggy Rathmann (Putnam, 1995)

Police Cat by Enid Hinkes (Albert Whitman & Co., 2005)

The Police Cloud by Christoph Niemann (Schwartz & Wade, 2007)

Policeman Small by Lois Lenski (Random House, 2001)

The Post Office

Flat Stanley by Jeff Brown (HarperCollins, 2006)

Harvey Hare, Postman Extraordinaire by Bernadette Watts (North-South, 1999).

Mail Carriers by Dee Ready (Bridgestone Books, 1998)

The Medical Clinic

Big Book of the Human Body (DK Publishing, 2006)

Me and My Amazing Body by Joan Sweeney (Dragonfly Books, 2000)

My Friend the Doctor by Joanna Cole (HarperCollins, 2005)

What to Expect When You Go to the Doctor by Heidi Murkoff (HarperFestival, 2000)

The Dental Clinic

The Berenstain Bears Visit the Dentist by Stan and Jan Berenstain (Random House, 1981)

Doctor De Soto by William Steig (Farrar, Straus and Giroux, 1990)

Going to the Dentist by Dawn Sirett (DK Publishing, 2007)

How Many Teeth? by Paul Showers (HarperTrophy, 1991)

Look! My Tooth Is Loose! by Patricia Brennan Demuth (Grosset & Dunlap, 2002)

Throw Your Tooth on the Roof: Tooth Traditions from Around the World by Selby Beeler (Houghton Mifflin, 2001)

The Animal Health Clinic

Bark, George by Jules Feiffer (HarperCollins Publishers, 1999)

My Cat Is Going to the Dogs by Mike Thaler (Troll Communications, 1999)

Landfill and Recycling Center

I Drive a Garbage Truck by Sarah Bridges (Picture Window Books, 2005)

Smash! Mash! Crash! There Goes the Trash! by Barbara Odanaka (Margaret K. McElderry Books, 2006)

Something from Nothing by Phoebe Gilman (Scholastic Canada, 2008)

Where Does the Garbage Go? by Paul Showers (HarperCollins Publishers, 1994)

Construction Sites

Construction Zone by Tana Hoban (Greenwillow, 1997)

The Lot at the End of My Block by Kevin Lewis (Hyperion, 2001)

Mike Mulligan and His Steam Shovel by Virginia Lee Burton (Houghton Mifflin, 2007)

One Big Building: A Counting Book About Construction by Michael Dahl (Picture Window Books, 2004)

Tools by Taro Miura (Chronicle, 2006)

Restaurants

Dim Sum for Everyone! by Grace Lin (Knopf, 2001)

Good Enough to Eat: A Kid's Guide to Food and Nutrition by Lizzy Rockwall (HarperCollins, 1999)

Gregory the Terrible Eater by Mitchell Sharmat (Simon & Schuster, 1984)

Froggy Eats Out by Jonathan London (Viking Juvenile, 2001)

Transportation

The Adventures of Taxi Dog by Debra and Sal Barracca (Puffin, 2000)

Don't Let the Pigeon Drive the Bus by Mo Willems (Hyperion, 2003)

Lisa's Airplane Trip by Anne Gutman (Knopf, 2001)

The Little Airplane by Lois Lenski (Random House, 2003)

Moon Plane by Peter McCarty (Henry Holt, 2006)

Next Stop! by Sarah Ellis (Fitzhenry and Whiteside, 2000)

The Subway Mouse by Barbara Reid (Scholastic, 2005)

Subway Sparrow by Leyla Torres (Farrar, Strauss and Giroux, 1993)

My Neighborhood

Materials

- Card stock
- Chart paper
- Crayons or markers
- Digital camera
- Large sheet of craft paper
- Picture books as listed

Getting Ready

- Take pictures of your school and homes and businesses in the school neighborhood. Develop the photos in a 5" x 7" (13 cm x 18 cm) or larger format.
- If you prefer not to take pictures, copy the chosen building fronts and places in the neighborhood (found on pages 8–15) onto card stock and cut them out.

A Neighborhood Is . . .

Each neighborhood is unique and different from other neighborhoods because of the people and/or businesses located there. Who are the people and what are the places in your school neighborhood? Read aloud *The Best Town in the World* by Byrd Baylor (Aladdin, 1986) or *Town Mouse, Country Mouse* by Jan Brett (Putnam Juvenile, 1994) and then have children talk about why they think their school neighborhood is a special place. Show the photos of neighborhood businesses and public places to the class. Have children individually tell about their favorite places and explain why they selected them.

Every neighborhood is full of people who help make the neighborhood go. School bus driver, street sweeper, baker, auto mechanic, and plumber are just a few examples of important jobs that people in the community do. Read aloud *Community Helpers from A to Z* by Bobbie Kalman (Crabtree Publishing Company, 1998) and discuss the different kinds of jobs featured in the book to prepare children for the following activity.

Make a simple map of your school neighborhood or use the one you have prepared as suggested on page 5. Tape a large sheet of craft paper on the floor or attach it to a bulletin board. Begin the activity with the class by drawing the road(s). Place or draw a picture of your school in the appropriate spot and then have children help you position on the map the remaining photographs of recognizable buildings. Talk about each picture and, if appropriate, what kind of jobs workers do there. On a large sheet of chart paper, have children help you list all of the different occupations of people who work in your neighborhood or community. Include as many people and places as you can think of and then consult a local phone directory for more ideas. (Note: Post the list and add to it as each theme in this resource book is studied.) Explain to children that they will be learning more about these featured places on the map during the next several weeks.

Helping Others

Materials

- Construction paper
- Crayons or markers
- Flowerpot or bucket
- Paper and pencil
- Picture books as listed
- Plaster of paris
- String and hole punch
- Tree branch

Getting Ready

- Set a dead tree branch in a pot or bucket and fill the container with plaster of paris so that the branch stands up on its own like a tree.
- To make a mitten-shaped pocket for each child, stack two sheets of colored construction paper and cut out a mitten shape. Staple around the edges, leaving an opening at the wrist. Punch a hole in one corner near the opening of the mitten and tie a string through the hole. Label each mitten with a child's name.

- Write personal notes to the children, highlighting the ways you have seen them being kind and helpful to others. Roll up each note and stick it inside the child's mitten. Hang the mittens on the tree branch.

Anyone can make a positive impact in her community. Even young children can learn to look beyond themselves to help people around them. As a class, make a list of things you might do to help out in your neighborhood. See *Do Something in Your Community* by Amanda Rondeau (ABDO, 2004) for some suggestions or include some of the following ideas in your list:

- Have a food drive for a local food bank.
- Collect spare change and donate the proceeds to purchase a book for your local library.
- Clean up litter.
- Help someone else do a job such as raking or carrying groceries.

Read aloud *The Mitten Tree* by Candace Christiansen (Fulcrum, 1997) and talk about how enjoyable it is to do something nice for someone else as a surprise. Have children write or dictate their public service ideas and then illustrate their papers. Compile the finished papers into a class book on neighborhood service.

Have children find the mittens labeled with their names on the classroom mitten tree. Take some time with each child to read the prepared note. You may wish to thank the child for being such a great neighbor. Let children personalize their mittens by decorating them with crayons or markers and then hang the mittens on the tree branch to create a classroom display.

Number Walk

Materials

- Clipboard, paper, and pencil
- Digital camera
- Picture books as listed

Getting Ready

- Decide beforehand which things you would like children to notice on the walk. Record those items on the paper. If needed, refer to the list in the activity directions (at right) for additional ideas.

The best way to explore your school neighborhood is to take the class on a walk. Obviously, there are many different things to observe. Depending on the maturity of the group, you might consider concentrating on one thing each time the class takes a stroll. To prepare for the walk, read aloud *City 123* by Zoran Milich (Kids Can Press, 2007) or another book about the numbers all around us. Explain to children that they are going to take an excursion through the neighborhood and look for specific things. When it is time to take off on the walk, sing the song "The Children Go Marching" (see page 33) with the children. Then, have fun trying to spy various things that you recorded on your list. Ideas for things to identify include the following:

- A pattern
- Something "big" or something "little"
- The number 2 or another numeral
- Numbers in order (i.e., 1, 2, 3)
- Something above the children's heads
- Counting five cars and then one more
- The number of wheels found on a car and the number on a motorcycle
- Estimating and then counting how many steps between landmarks.

As children find each item on your list, take a photograph of it (or help a child take the photograph) and note it on the clipboard. When everyone has returned to the classroom, record the numbers and items found on a large sheet of chart paper and print copies of the pictures. During group time, let children match the pictures to the list of items that were found during the walk. You may wish to extend the lesson by encouraging children to look around the classroom for other numbers. Also, have them think about numbers that they can find in their homes, backyards, at the park, and so on.

Alternatively, children may enjoy looking for letters, shapes, or colors while walking through the neighborhood. Read aloud the following books: *C Is for City* by Nikki Grimes (Lothrop, Lee & Shepard, 1995), *The City ABC Book* by Zoran Milich (Kids Can Press, 2002), or *City Colors* by Zoran Milich (Kids Can Press, 2006) and then use the books to introduce future excursions.

The Children Go Marching

(Sing to the tune of "The Ants Go Marching")

The children go marching one by one, hurrah, hurrah.
The children go marching one by one, hurrah, hurrah.
The children go marching one by one, the last one in line twiddles his thumbs,
And they all go marching down to the ground to get out of the rain,
BOOM, BOOM, BOOM.
(As everyone sings the last line of the verse, have the child who is first in the marching line move to the end to allow the next child to be the leader.)

Repeat verses with the following numbers:
The children go marching two by two, . . . the last one in line ties her shoe . . .
The children go marching three by three, . . . the last one in line climbs a tree . . .
The children go marching four by four, . . . the last one in line shuts the door . . .
The children go marching five by five, . . . the last one in line finds a beehive . . .
The children go marching six by six, . . . the last one in line picks up sticks . . .
The children go marching seven by seven, . . . the last one in line looks up to heaven . . .
The children go marching eight by eight, . . . the last one in line shuts the gate . . .
The children go marching nine by nine, . . . the last one in line says, "I'm fine" . . .
The children go marching ten by ten, . . . the last one in line says, "Let's do it again" . . .

Give Me a Sign

Materials

• Construction paper
• Crayons or markers
• Long dowels or yardsticks/metersticks
• Picture books as listed

There are signs all around a neighborhood. Some give us information and some warn us. Show children the pictures in the book *City Signs* by Zoran Milich (Kids Can Press, 2002) or *I Read Signs* by Tana Hoban (Greenwillow, 1983). Other books you might like to share with the class are those written by Mary Hill (Children's Press, 2003): *Signs on the Road*, *Signs at the Store*, *Signs at School*, *Signs at the Park*, and *Signs at the Airport*. Brainstorm with children to make a list of the numerous kinds of signs that are visible in your community. Wrap up the activity by having children create their own street signs on sheets of construction paper. Tape the signs to dowels or yardsticks/metersticks and have children carry them in a sign parade around the classroom or display them on classroom walls. Be sure to look for street signs, traffic signs, information signs, and building signs when taking children on walks in the neighborhood. If possible, take photos of signs for class discussions.

Materials

• Picture books as listed

Getting Ready

• Prepare a letter to parents requesting that children bring food or prizes to share with the class.

Block Party

Neighbors also gather together to get to know one another and have fun. National Night Out (celebrated the first Tuesday in August) is a special evening when people gather outside in their neighborhoods to meet one another and celebrate their communities. Read aloud the book *Everybody Brings Noodles* by Nora Dooley (Carolrhoda Books, 2005) or *Sweet Dream Pie* by Audrey Wood (Blue Sky Press, 1998). Talk about all the fun experiences children may have when socializing with neighbors. Share with the children a memory of your own childhood neighborhood or a story about your current one.

Have children help you plan a school "block party." Send home the parent note inviting each child to bring an item for the classroom's neighborhood block party. Items can be either foods (follow your school's guidelines for serving food's in the classroom) or trinkets for prizes. On the designated day, celebrate by playing games and sharing the items brought by children.

Extend the lesson by talking about what it means to be a good neighbor. Have children draw pictures and make greeting cards that you can take to a neighbor near your school.

Kindergarten Corner:
My Neighborhood, Then and Now

How has your neighborhood changed in 100 years? To prepare for this lesson, check with your local historical society chapter, library, or city hall to locate old pictures and historical information.

Discuss with children the kinds of things that may have happened many years ago in the very spot where they are sitting. Perhaps the area was a colonial street, a farm, or a forest. Read aloud *Window* by Jeannie Baker (Walker Books Ltd., 2002), a wordless book illustrating how an area changed from a rural setting to an urban community.

Extend the lesson by letting children make a poster or diorama of their neighborhood. One panel should depict what the area looked like before people lived there while the other side shows what it looks like now.

Materials

• Picture books as listed
• Shoe box or construction paper and craft materials

All About Me

I Like Me

Materials

- Paper and crayons
- Picture books as listed
- Small box with lid
- Small mirror
- Stapler and scissors
- Wrapping paper

Getting Ready

- Cover a small box and lid with attractive wrapping paper.
- Attach the mirror to the interior bottom of the box.
- Make a copy of page 39 for each child. Refer to the activity directions for assembling the booklet.

Each one of us is unique and special in certain ways. To help children think differently about their physical traits and to celebrate their own and one another's differences, read aloud *I Like Me* by Nancy Carlson (Puffin, 1990) or Allia Zobel-Nolen's *What I Like About Me* (Reader's Digest, 2005) or *What I Do Best* (Reader's Digest, 2006). Talk about the children in the books and the things they love about themselves. Solicit responses from children in your class about their personal interests or hobbies or something about themselves that they like.

Show children the box you have decorated. Explain that it contains something very special and that you will let each child peek inside it, but everyone must keep what they see a secret. (You will have to give several reminders about this as children take turns looking in the box.) Choose one child to come to the front of the class. Say to the child that there is something very special and very beautiful inside the box and personalize your comments by describing one of the child's personality traits, such as "This special thing in the box is a good listener." Then, invite the child to open the box and look inside where he will see his face reflected in the mirror. Repeat with each child until everyone in the class has had a turn.

Let children create *I'm Special* booklets. Make a copy of the child outline on page 39 for each child in the class. Have each child color a self-portrait to make the front cover. Stack several sheets of plain copy paper behind each colored outline and staple all papers together at the top of the booklet shape. Cut around the outline to create a person-shaped booklet. Then, spend some one-on-one time with each child to generate a list of personality strengths. Write each idea on a separate page of the booklet. Read the book together when it is completed. Send a note home with the booklets, encouraging each child's parents to help their child complete more booklet pages.

Introduce Yourself

Getting Ready

- Clear a large area in the classroom so that children can move about freely without running into furniture.

Here is a fun way for children to practice the social skill of introducing themselves to others. Explain to the class that when a person meets someone else for the first time, it is important to make an introduction, which involves looking at the other person's eyes and shaking hands (typically using the right hands). The two people then introduce themselves by saying, "Hello, my name is _____." Demonstrate by introducing yourself to each child. (Be aware that certain cultures consider it disrespectful to look directly at another person. If this is the case for some children in your classroom, you will want to make accommodations for them.)

Practice introductions by having the children move about the room until you give a signal, such as ringing a bell. When children hear the signal, they should stop moving, find a child who is close to them, practice shaking hands, and take turns saying, "Hello, my name is _____." After everyone has practiced these steps several times, continue the activity by demonstrating how to introduce a third party. Ask one child to stand at your side. For example, take Megan's hand and lead her to another child in the class. As you greet the second child, introduce Megan to the child by saying, "Hello, _____. This is my friend Megan." Have the children form teams of two members and practice introducing one another to other teams in class.

Extend the activity by singing "Rig-a-Jig-Jig," an English folk song (lyrics provided below), as children prance around the room. When everyone sings the words "a friend of mine I chanced to meet," have children stop, greet a friend with a handshake, join both hands with their new partners, and dance together while singing until the end of the song. Repeat the activity and let children find a new friend each time the song is sung. Alternatively, change the words to reflect actions other than walking, such as hopping, skipping, jumping, etc., to keep children engaged in the activity.

Traditional/Adapted

Rig-a-Jig-Jig

As I was walking down the street,

Down the street, down the street.

A friend of mine I chanced to meet,

Hello, hello, hello.

A rig-a-jig-jig and away we go,

Away we go, away we go.

Rig-a-jig-jig and away we go,

Hi-ho, Hi-ho, Hi-ho.

Materials

• Digital camera
• Marker and glue
• Poster board

Getting Ready

• Take photographs of
  the children's faces and
  make multiple copies
  of the prints.
• Prepare the poster
  board by drawing grid
  lines for the graph.

Materials

• Cardboard
• Construction paper
• Craft paper
• Digital camera
• Markers, crayons,
  scissors, and glue

Materials

• Baking cup liners
• Ingredients needed to
  make muffins
• Mixing bowl
• Muffin tins
• Picture book as listed
• Spoon

Making a Class Pictograph

An engaging way to practice counting items and observing details is to create a pictograph with the class. Choose a topic that would apply to all children, such as eye color. Label the categories by writing the physical characteristics, such as brown, blue, green, etc. Then, use the photos of children's faces to fill in the graph, rather than coloring in each space on the grid. Discuss as a class, for example, which children have brown eyes and have them come forward to glue their pictures on the grid in the corresponding row or column. Continue the activity with the remaining eye colors. Other ideas of things to graph include hair color, height, how the children get to school, etc.

Growing "Flower Cuties" Bulletin Board

Comparing children's heights can be a lot of fun. To make this special height chart, cover a wall with craft paper. Use enough paper so that the top edge of the background paper is slightly higher than the tallest child in class. Draw a simple flower pattern about 12" (30 cm) in diameter on a piece of cardboard and cut it out to make a flower template. Have each child use the template to trace a flower on a sheet of colored construction paper and cut it out. If you have taken pictures of the children, make copies of the photographs and distribute them. Otherwise, the children may draw their faces on paper. Finish the flowers by cutting around the faces and gluing them onto the flowers. Line up the children along the craft paper to measure how tall each child is. Position the top of the flower cutout on the spot that indicates the child's height and glue it in place. Then, let each child paint a green stem from the flower to the floor and add some leaves if desired. Repeat with all of the children until you have a full flower garden of growing cuties!

Friendship Muffins

Purchase a favorite muffin mix and make muffins in the classroom. (NOTE: Follow your school's guidelines for serving foods in the classroom.) Give each child an ingredient to pour into the bowl or let children help you stir or pour the batter into the muffin tins. As the muffins bake in the oven, read aloud *39 Uses for a Friend* by Harriet Ziefert (G.P. Putnam's Sons 2001). Make a list of "friend words" like help, share, and so on. No doubt, everyone will be eager to share a story of a joyous time being with friends. While children eat their muffins, point out that each friend's contribution helped to make the muffins very tasty.

Dramatic Play Center: Birthday Party!

Materials

- Birthday banners and streamers
- Plastic cups and plates
- Pretend party food such as cupcakes and ice cream
- Wrapping paper, tape, boxes, ribbon, construction paper, crayons, and scissors

After announcing to the class that there will be a birthday celebration, let children decide how to decorate the designated area. The children will enjoy preparing for the birthday party by decorating the play area with banners and streamers. Let them wrap toys from the classroom for gifts and make birthday cards with construction paper and crayons. If balloons are inflated, be sure to follow school guidelines. Provide children with play food such as cupcakes that can be served to their guests during the party.

Kindergarten Corner: People Diagrams

Materials

- 12" x 18" (30 cm x 46 cm) sheets of manila craft paper
- Colorful construction paper
- Crayons or markers
- Glue

Getting Ready

- Cut out construction paper circles in two sizes: 4" (10 cm) and 6" (15 cm).

To help children understand how each person is connected to different people, create a visual tool with circles. Demonstrate [...] as an example. Glue a 6" (15 cm) circle in the middle of a piece [...] Draw a self-portrait and write your name in that circle. Show [...] your paper and talk about how this circle is nice, but it is also v[...] Explain that this circle "needs" other circles to help it to be happy. [...] at a time, discuss all of the different people including family, friends, sports teams, book clubs, play groups, etc., that you interact with. As you talk about each group, fill in a 4" (10 cm) circle by writing the names and drawing pictures (stick figures) of individuals that represent the group. Glue a "family circle" on the paper as you talk about the people in your family. Glue a "friend circle" on the paper as you talk about your friends. Continue with other smaller circles as desired and then use a marker or crayon to draw a line connecting the larger circle to each smaller circle.

Give each child a sheet of paper, a 6" (15 cm) paper circle, and several 4" (10 cm) paper circles. Let them create their own diagrams of all of the people to whom they are connected. If needed, help children identify and write down the name of each group.

To the teacher: Have the child draw pictures and write a few words to finish the sentence on each page.

This is my family. One thing we like to do together is . . .

3

This is my friend. One thing we like to do together is . . .

4

To the teacher: Have the child draw pictures and write a few words to finish the sentence on each page.

These are things that I like . . .

5

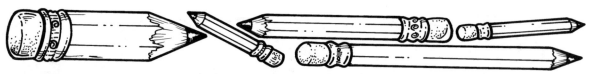

Something else you should know
about me is . . .

6

My Home

A House Is Made of . . .

Materials

- Assortment of building supplies and a few unrelated items
- Chart paper and marker
- Large cardboard box

Getting Ready

- Gather samples of materials for building a house. Be sure to solicit parents to help locate samples of materials, too.
- Place all of the items in a large cardboard box. Also, include a few items unrelated to building materials in the box.

What materials are used to make a house? Brainstorm answers with the class. As children call out ideas, record them on the chart paper. When all of the ideas have been written down, have children remove the objects from the box one at a time to see if any of them are items that were suggested by the class. Use descriptive words to explain each object and discuss as a group how the item may be used. Talk about how building a house takes a lot of time and a lot of workers to complete the project. Also, discuss how some materials are good for building the exterior of a house and some are appropriate for the interior construction. Whenever an item that does not belong in the group of materials is discovered by the children, set it aside. Place all of the building materials on a table with a small scale, measuring tape, and magnifying glasses so that children can examine them thoroughly at a later time.

Big House, Little House

Materials

- Pencils and crayons
- Picture books as listed
- Stapler

Getting Ready

- Prepare the booklet *Is This My House?* for each child. Directions are provided on pages 49 and 50.

There are many different kinds of houses: apartments, townhouses, condominiums, single-story houses, three- or four-story houses, split-level entry houses, houses built out of mud or grass, and so on. Where you live is what mainly determines the kind of home you live in. Read aloud *The Little House* by Virginia Lee Burton (Houghton Mifflin, 1978), *Houses and Homes* by Ann Morris (HarperTrophy, 1995), or *Houses* by Gallimard Jeunesse and Claude Delasfosse (Scholastic, 1998). Talk about the different kinds of houses depicted in the books and the different resources used to build them. For example, people who live in parts of the world where certain building materials are scarce may build their houses out of native plants.

Regardless of what kinds of houses people live in, homes are built for comfort and shelter. Read aloud *A House Is a House for Me* by Mary Ann Hoberman (Puffin, 2007) or *A House for Hermit Crab* by Eric Carle (Aladdin, 2005) and discuss what makes a home. Give each child a copy of the *Is This My House?* booklet. Let children draw self-portraits to complete their booklets, as directed on pages 49 and 50.

Building a House with Sticks or Bricks

Materials

- 3 different hats (cowboy, baseball, construction)
- Copies of page 48
- Crayons and glue
- Large brown grocery bags (or pillow cases)
- Pink, brown, and black sheets of construction paper
- Knee-high length of nylon stocking
- Newspaper
- Red construction paper cut into 1/2" x 3/4" (13 mm x 19 mm) rectangles for "bricks"
- Safety pin
- Small twigs
- Straw or cut raffia
- Tape

Getting Ready

- Create three pig headbands by cutting strips of pink construction paper. Staple each strip's ends together to create a loop. Cut two small pig ears out of the construction paper and attach them to each headband.
- Cut three 2" (5 cm) pink circles. Make pig noses by drawing two dots on each circle.
- Create a similar headband from brown construction paper for the wolf. Cut out two wolf ears and attach them to the headband.
- Cut a 2" (5 cm) circle from black paper for the wolf's nose.
- Make a slit (large enough for a child's head to pass through) along the top of each of the grocery bags (or pillow cases). To make two armholes, cut a 6" (15 cm) slit along each side of the bag, beginning about 2" (5 cm) from the top.
- Cut three spiral pig tails out of pink paper. Tape one end of each spiral to the back of each pig's grocery bag.
- Stuff the nylon stocking with crumpled newspaper to make the wolf's tail. Place a strip of tape across the middle of the back of the grocery bag to reinforce the spot. Use the safety pin to attach the stuffed stocking to the back of the bag through the reinforcing tape.

Act It Out!

As a class, act out the story of the "Three Little Pigs." To set the scene, choose three children to be the little pigs. Slip the white garbage bags over their heads (make sure the tails are in back) and have them slide their arms through the slits on the sides. Place the headbands with the pig ears on their heads and tape a pig nose to each child's nose. Ask each little pig to wear a different hat. Dress another child as the wolf in the prepared black garbage bag. Place the wolf headband on that child's head and tape the black circle to the child's nose.

Have children take turns being the characters in the story of the three pigs. Talk about which house was the strongest and why it did not blow down like the other houses.

Materials

- Black craft paper
- Collage materials (chenille stems, feathers, dried beans, etc.)
- Craft glue and tape
- Crayons and markers
- Index cards
- Nature materials (sticks, twigs, grasses, dried leaves, etc.)
- Shoe boxes
- Small plastic people

Act It Out! (Continued)

To extend the activity, make three copies of the house on page 48 for each child. Children should cut out their houses and glue them side by side on large sheets of construction paper. Have children glue straw on the first house, small twigs on the second house, and small, rectangular, construction paper "bricks" on the third house. Encourage them to draw additional details on their papers, such as the three pigs, the wolf, and trees. Then, have them write "No" above the straw and stick houses and "Yes" above the house of bricks. When finished with the project, invite children to pick up where the story ended and write or dictate "what happened next" on a separate piece of paper. Attach the dictated story to the picture.

Shoe Box Town ✳

It's easy to convert shoe boxes into houses, townhouses, and apartment buildings to make a miniature neighborhood. Give each child a shoe box and a large selection of collage and craft materials. Then, turn the boxes into "homes" by letting children decorate them as they wish. When the creations are finished, have everyone sit in a circle around the "shoe box homes." Identify the materials that were used to make the models.

Extend the lesson by arranging the shoe box houses along a "street." Cut a long strip of black craft paper to create a road and tape it to the floor. Line up all of the houses along the road. Have children choose a name for your class's street, write it on a street sign, and place it at the end of the paper. Give each child a small index card. Challenge children to work together as a group to assign each house a building number. Write those numbers on the cards. Fold another index card in half lengthwise and write each child's name on one side. Set the cards on top of the houses to identify the owners of the homes.

Pick out a small plastic person and give it a name, such as "Amber." Introduce Amber to the children. Tell them that Amber would like to visit a few homes on their street. Have children take turns moving Amber from house to house based on simple directions that you give. For example, tell the first child that Amber wants to go to the third house on the street. The child would then move the figure to that house. Another child may be instructed to look for a particular house number, color, or building material.

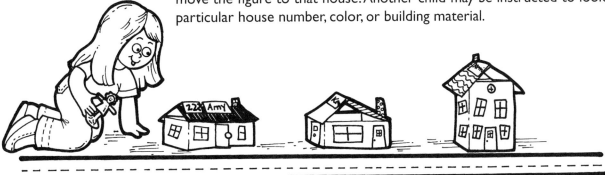

Materials

- 2 large sheets of craft paper or poster board
- Colorful construction paper
- Home improvement and decorating magazines
- Markers and tape
- Picture book as listed

Getting Ready

- Cut out several pictures of furniture and household appliances from magazines.
- Cut construction paper into various sizes of squares and rectangles (these will be the "rooms" in the house).
- Copy page 48 for children.

Materials

- Spray bottle filled with water
- Cloth rags
- Cleaning items (squeegee, mop, dustpan, broom, vacuum cleaner, etc.)

Room for All

Homes have many different rooms, each one with a specific purpose or use. For example, a kitchen is used for storing, preparing, and eating food. Read aloud the book *My Home: Walls, Doors, Ceilings, and Floors* by Lisa Bullard (Picture Window Books, 2003) or another book about homes. Tell children that you need help in building a house. Ask them to describe the rooms in their houses. While talking about the rooms, create a simple diagram of a house by taping construction paper squares onto a large sheet of craft paper. (Each square or rectangle represents one room.) As you "build" each room, discuss its use and the kinds of furniture or other appliances that might be located there. Let children place pictures of household items in the appropriate rooms.

Give each child a copy of page 48. Let each child select either the house or apartment building picture and color and glue it on a sheet of construction paper. Direct children to dictate or write a story about their favorite at-home activities.

Extend the lesson by letting children make picture diagrams of their homes.

Knock, Knock, Cleaning Service

Homes get dirty because people and pets live in them. It's the whole family's job to keep their home clean and tidy. Sometimes, a home needs a little extra care and that's when we call in a cleaning service! Talk about all of the different kinds of cleaning jobs that must be done in a home. Brainstorm with children a list of these jobs, including cleaning windows, vacuuming, sweeping, scrubbing floors, washing the tub, etc. Let children become the "cleaning crew" and show how to use the provided tools. After a child has demonstrated each job, have children mime the actions as you sing the following song together:

Let's Clean

(Sing to the tune of "Mulberry Bush")

This is the way we [scrub the floor],

[Scrub the floor], [scrub the floor].

This is the way we [scrub the floor]

Early in the morning.

Repeat the song using other actions for cleaning.

Dramatic Play Center: My Own House ✳

Materials

- Assortment of items to create an area where children may pretend to be in a house
- Markers, crayons, and other art materials

Set up a special "house" area by providing lots of different household items for imaginative free play. Plastic tools, appliances, cleaning tools, household goods, plastic food, and empty food containers are all great options.

Bring in large appliance boxes or cover tables with blankets to create a "neighborhood of houses." Children may use art materials to decorate the houses.

Community Connections ✳

Invite one or more of the following people to visit your classroom: home builder, real estate agent, house cleaner, handyman repair person, lawn service person, landscaper, painter, plumber, electrician, tree trimmer, carpet layer, etc. Additional information about inviting visitors is provided on page 6.

Kindergarten Corner: Communities ✳

Materials

- Construction paper, crayons, and markers
- Picture books as listed

What kind of community do you live in? There are three basic kinds of communities: urban, rural, and suburban. Urban communities are best described as "city life." Single family homes are rare, and most people live in apartment buildings or condominiums. Rural communities are best described as "country life." There are very few people living in those areas. People who live on farms or ranches are a good example of rural living. Suburban communities are places where many families live close together, usually in single-family homes or townhouses. Goods and services are close by and easily accessible.

Talk with the children about what kind of home community they live in. Share information about many different kinds of places, such as living on a river, in the desert, etc. Use any of the following Communities series (or similar) books to illustrate the different kinds of places where people live. Discuss the advantages and disadvantages that living in different places might bring.

Living in a Desert by Jan Kottke (Children's Press, 2000)
Living in a Rain Forest by Joanne Winne (Children's Press, 2000)
Living near a River by Joanne Winne (Children's Press, 2000)
Living on a Mountain by Joanne Winne (Children's Press, 2000)
Living on a Plain by Joanne Winne (Children's Press, 2000)

Give each child a large sheet of construction paper. Direct children to divide their papers in half by folding them down the middle. Each child should label the top of the left panel "Where I Live." The top of the right panel should be labeled "Where I Would Like to Live." Have children use crayons and markers to draw pictures of their present homes and dream homes on their papers.

House and Apartment Building Patterns *(Refer to directions on pages 45 and 46.)*

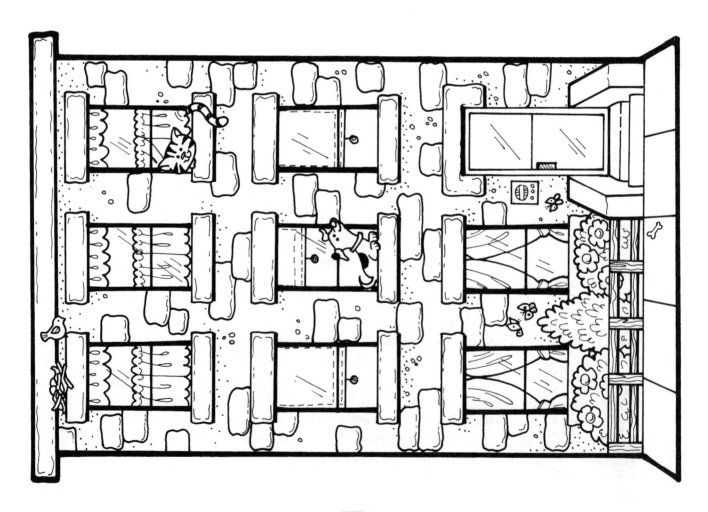

To the teacher: Make one copy of the booklet (pages 49 and 50) for each child. Cut out each page along the dashed lines. Collate the booklet pages and staple them together. On page 2, have the child draw a self-portrait shown sitting in the nest.

Name:

Is this my house? How can it be?
This is a house that you see in a tree.

2

To the teacher: On page 3, have the child draw a self-portrait shown sitting in the doghouse. On page 4, have the child draw a self-portrait shown standing by the door.

Is this my house?
If you haven't
guessed yet,
this is a house
that is a home
for a pet.

3

Is this my house?
It's better than
the rest.
It's the place
where I live and
I like it the best!

4

My Backyard

Materials

- Chart paper and marker
- Crayons
- Food scraps (apple, orange, cookie, etc.)
- Magnifying glasses
- Nonfood items (twig, rock, eraser, etc.)
- Paper
- Picture books as listed
- Shovel

Getting Ready

- Cut several sheets of blank paper in half lengthwise.
- Stack three or four prepared strips and fold them in half vertically to make a booklet for each child.
- Staple the booklet along the folded edge.
- Write "My Wildlife Neighbors" on the front of each booklet.

Bugs, Slugs, and Other "Neighbors"

Which animals that are smaller than your hand can you see in your backyard? Brainstorm with children a list of those animals and write them on chart paper. Read aloud *In My Backyard* by Margriet Ruurs (Tundra, 2007) or *The Snail's Spell* by Joanne Ryder (Puffin, 1988) to learn more about some animals. As a class, discuss the different types of small animals and point out which ones live in different terrains and climates.

Give each child a magnifying glass, a crayon, and a prepared booklet and then head outdoors with the class to look for small creatures in your school's "backyard." (Be sure to emphasize that the creatures should be observed only and not touched.) Encourage children to look under rocks, on plant leaves, in the center of flowers, and on tree bark for small creatures. Remind children to look overhead on tree branches, too. Perhaps you will find evidence such as a snail's trail, a damaged leaf, or a spider's web. You may also wish to turn over a shovelful of dirt to see what lives just underground. Invite children to draw pictures of the things they find. When back in the classroom, have children "write" about their discoveries.

Wrap up the lesson about backyard "neighbors" by setting out "fixin's" for a neighborhood bug party. Place a sheet of paper on the ground in an area that will not be disturbed by people. Have children help you choose several different items (include food and nonfood items) to place on the paper. As a group, predict which items will attract insects. Then, check the paper periodically to see if any bugs showed up for the party.

Materials

- Index cards
- Planting materials
- Seeds to plant

Getting Ready

- Glue a few seeds from each selected packet on a file card.

My Garden

Have children gather around you and look at one of the seed cards you have prepared. Say to children, "What might grow from the seed?" While they examine the seeds and try to answer your question, you may wish to give clues. For example, you might say, "This seed grows into something that is very tall" or "This seed grows into something that smells sweet." Once the children have made a few guesses about the seeds, show them the seed packet.

Give each child one or two seeds to plant in a cup, pot, or in a shared garden space. Water the soil when needed. Over the next weeks, watch the seedlings emerge from the soil and become full-grown plants.

Materials

- Assorted items used or found in a backyard
- Dirt (not potting soil) and water
- Drop cloths and paint cover-ups
- Fast-start grass seeds
- Finger-paint paper
- Large shallow pans
- Spray bottle and water

Getting Ready

- Mix the dirt and water to make mud in a paint-like consistency.
- Pour the mud into a large shallow pan that will accommodate the tools and other backyard items.
- Set the tools and the pans of mud "paint" on a covered table.

Materials

- Assorted items for hiding in sand (small plastic bugs, toys, etc.)
- Sand
- Sand table or large container
- Small buckets
- Small toy shovels

Getting Ready

- Fill the sand table or a large container with sand.
- Hide completely several selected items in the sand.

Backyard Art

Give each child a large sheet of paper. Using the mud as paint and the provided tools, have children make prints on their papers. To foster logical thinking skills, direct children to make prints of things from nature (flowers, leaves, rocks, twigs, etc.) on one-half of the paper and prints of things that are manufactured (shovel, hand rake, etc.) on the other half.

Perhaps the children will be eager to draw favorite backyard scenes on their papers using only their fingers. While they create their "masterpieces," encourage them to talk about how the mud feels, smells, and looks. This is a wonderful opportunity to introduce new words. When the drawings are complete, sprinkle fast-start grass seeds on the mud. Over the next few days, keep the mud moist by spraying water on it and watch the pictures sprout!

Sandbox Treasure Sort

It's fun to search for buried treasures. If you have a large container or a sand table, find some interesting items to bury in the sand. When it is time to hunt for treasures, have children place each found item in a bucket. When they have finished digging and searching for the "treasures," let them sort the found items according to one attribute, such as size or color. To tailor the sorting activities, change the items hidden in the sand frequently. Topic may include items with names that begin with the letter *F* (fish, fence, numeral 4, etc.), animals, and so on.

Dramatic Play Center: Backyard Tree House

Materials

- Bucket
- Child-sized gardening tools
- Flowerpots and dried beans or florist's foam
- Garden hose (a short section that is clean)
- Large furniture box
- Plastic bugs and other creatures
- Rope
- Silk flowers and artificial plants

It's easy to change your dramatic play center into a backyard "tree house." Bring in a large furniture box and cut it down so that its height is about a child's height. Cut out one side of the box to make an opening for children to step into. If there is time, let them paint the box to decorate it. Arrange artificial trees or plants near your tree house to make it feel as if it is hidden in a large tree. Attach the rope to the bucket so that children can pretend to use it to raise and lower items into the tree house.

The "backyard" would not be complete without a flower garden. Place flowerpots filled with dried beans or chunks of florist's foam, silk flowers, and small gardening tools along one side of the play area for gardening activities. Use a short section of an old garden hose to get "water" to the garden and provide a storage system that requires children to wind up the hose after it is used. Arrange bugs and other plastic critters under rocks, behind objects, on top of the tree house, and so on. The area is now ready for lots of engaging play!

Community Connections

Invite a landscape specialist or plant nursery manager to visit your classroom and share about different flowers, shrubs, and trees that grow well in your location. You may also consider inviting a wildlife hobbyist who can share ideas for attracting butterflies and birds to a backyard or show pictures of birds that live in your geographical region. Additional information about inviting visitors into the classroom is provided on page 6.

Kindergarten Corner: Looking Back in Time

Materials

- Crayons or markers
- Large sheets of white construction paper
- Picture books as listed

Have you ever wondered what the area known as your backyard looked like many years ago? Read aloud *Window* by Jeannie Baker (Greenwillow, 1991) or *The Backyard* by John Collier (Viking, 1993) and then discuss what the children learned from the book. Visit your local library or historical society to locate old pictures of your community from when it was first established. (This lesson is a continuation of the activity on page 34.) Have children imagine what their backyards might have looked like before present-day buildings were built. Ask them to draw pictures of their backyards and how that same area looked 100 years ago.

Backyard Bingo

Materials

- Colorful card stock
- Copier paper
- Scissors and glue
- Small bowl or zippered plastic bag
- Small pebbles

Getting Ready: Make one copy of the Backyard Bingo board (page 55) on colorful card stock and one enlarged copy (125 percent) of the small bingo icons (page 56) on copier paper for each player. Also make one additional copy of the bingo icons on card stock for the caller. Cut out the picture icons along the dashed lines. To make the game boards, select pictures and arrange them randomly in the boxes provided (you will have more pictures than boxes on the bingo board) and then glue them in place. Repeat this step several times, arranging and gluing various pictures in the boxes so that several different bingo boards are assembled. It is recommended that you make one board for each child in the class or fewer boards if using them only during a small group activity. Place the set of bingo icons for the caller in a small bowl or zippered bag. Optional: Laminate the bingo boards and icon cards for durability.

To Play: Give each child a bingo board and a handful of small pebbles. Draw an icon card from the bowl or bag. Then, have children look for the card's matching picture on their boards and mark the correct box with a small pebble. Continue playing until one player has covered all of the boxes in a row or column.

File Folder Game: Wiggly Worms

Materials

- Colorful card stock
- Colorful file folder
- Craft knife
- Laminating material
- Markers
- Molding dough
- Scissors and glue
- Zippered plastic bag

Getting Ready: Make two copies of the bucket (page 57) and several copies of the alphabet cards (page 58) on colorful card stock. Determine which uppercase and lowercase alphabet letters you would like children to identify and make during the activity. Then, draw the chosen letters to look like worms on the cards and laminate them. Cut out the buckets and cards along the dashed lines.

Open a file folder and place it flat on a table. Glue one bucket on the right inside panel. On the second bucket, use a craft knife to cut along the provided dashed line to make a slit. Glue the top edge (above the slit), sides, and bottom half of the second bucket onto the left panel of the file folder. Close the folder and write the name "Wiggly Worms" on the tab or front panel. Laminate the prepared folder. Reopen the slit in the second bucket by cutting through the lamination along the dashed line to make a small pocket. Place the prepared cards in a zippered plastic bag and staple it to the folder. Store a can of molding dough with the file folder and game cards.

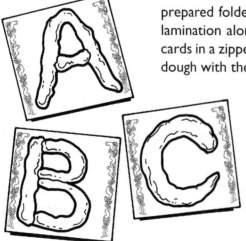

To Play:
1. Stack the wiggly worm cards near the file folder. Choose one card from the stack. Slip the card into the pocket in the bucket on the left side of the file folder.
2. Using the molding dough, roll small pieces of dough into worm shapes. Then, shape the "worms" to form the chosen letter on the "empty" bucket on the right.

Backyard Bingo

Backyard Bingo Icons *(Refer to directions on page 54.)*

Pictures: Row 1—sunshine, leaf, acorns, pine tree, palm tree; Row 2—tree, trash can, flowers, bug, snake; Row 3—worm, cat, dog, frog, turtle; Row 4—fence, rocks, grasshopper, tricycle, bicycle; Row 5—snowman, bat and ball, garden hose, sprinkler, watering can; Row 6—rain, kite, bird, deer, sandbox

Wiggly Worms Bucket *(Refer to directions on page 54.)*

Wiggly Worms Alphabet Cards *(Refer to directions on page 54.)*

Materials

- Colorful card stock
- Marker
- Poster board
- Scissors

Getting Ready

- Using colorful card stock, make two copies of the picture cards on page 65.

The Park

Walk and Talk: Learning New Words

A playground or park is a shared community space where people can come and play. Many parks have play equipment such as swings, structures to climb, and slides, as well as benches and shady areas that people can use to relax. In some parks, there may also be sandboxes, water fountains, walking paths, recreational fields for soccer and/or baseball, and tennis courts. If you can take the children on a walking field trip to a park, bring along your prepared picture cards, poster board, and a marker. Alternatively, if it is not feasible to walk to a park, use the second set of cards and tape them individually to surfaces around the room for an imaginary visit.

Show one of the cards and have children identify the featured picture. Then, on your signal, let children race to the corresponding spot. Once everyone is there, have children brainstorm words that describe the play equipment or the kinds of actions that are performed at the designated location. For example, if the selected card features the swings, the children might call out words like *swing, forward, back, push, exciting,* etc. Write the words on the poster board and repeat the activity with a new card.

What Do You See?

While exploring a park or playground, direct children to sit in a circle, facing outward. Use the opening line of a familiar story, "Brown Bear, Brown Bear, what do you see?" but replace the words "brown bear" with one of the children's names. For example, if you say, "Keela, Keela, what do you see?" the child might respond, "I see a swing set (or another large object that is in that child's view) looking at me." Continue in this manner around the circle of children for a 360-degree panoramic view of the playground. Remind children that what they describe does not have to be an entire piece of equipment. It can be anything within their eyesight, such as a tree branch, a window on a building, a flower bed, large bushes, and so on. To change the children's views, have them lie on their tummies or on their backs.

Counting on the Playground ✳

Materials

- Scrap paper
- Markers
- Tape

There are different ways to find numbers on a playground. Perhaps your class has observed numerals on the sides of objects. Invite children to tell you about those numbers and then have them search the playground for more numbers. (There may be numerals in unusual places!) Next, explain to the class that the playground is full of things that can be counted. Have children work in teams. Give each team a different name, such as the Tigers or the Bumblebees. Assign one child to be the "coach" of each team. Have the other children be the team members. Give the coach a piece of paper (with a strip of tape attached), a marker, and the name of an object located on the playground (such as *tree, slide, flowers, sidewalk cracks,* etc.). The coach then tells his team how everyone is going to move to the chosen object. For example, the children may hop on one foot, walk backwards, or clap while walking. The team moves with the correct action to the designated object and prepares to count. For example, if the named object is "tree," the team would count the total number of trees there. If the designated object is "slide," the children could count the number of steps on the ladder. Have the coach record the number on the piece of paper and attach it to the selected object. Repeat the exercise so that each child in the team has an opportunity to be the coach.

What Will Happen if . . . ? ✳

Materials

- Beanbags
- Rubber balls

The playground is a great place to investigate science concepts, such as gravity and inertia. Before trying each of the following experiments (or others you come up with), have children predict what they think will happen. Then, perform the experiment and compare the predictions to the results. Encourage children to talk about what they observed. Be sure to include words that describe the equipment or the conditions. For example, you might say "The slide is made of metal (or plastic). It is very smooth."

Here are some experiment ideas:

- Place a beanbag in a swing and give it a big push. Then, do the same with a ball.
- Place a ball at the top of the slide. Then, do the same with a beanbag.
- Roll a ball across a sidewalk and then across a grassy or sandy area.
- Toss a beanbag in the air. Then, toss a ball in the air.

Ice Cream Sandwich Snack

Materials

- 3 flavors of ice cream
- Apron and paper hat
- Cookies
- Ice cream scoop
- Melted chocolate (optional)
- Music CD and player
- Paper napkins
- Plastic food server gloves
- Play money
- Rolling cart or wagon

Getting Ready

- Place the ice cream, scoop, cookies, paper napkins, and music player on a rolling cart or wagon.
- Wear the apron and paper hat to look like an ice cream vendor.

Here is a fun idea for a cool, refreshing snack. (NOTE: Follow your school's guidelines for serving foods in the classroom.) Prepare the children for snack time by having them wash their hands. When everyone is seated at a table, give each child some play money. Explain that you have a surprise. Play the music while you roll out your "ice-cream stand." When you reach the first child, stop the music and ask what flavor of ice cream sandwich the child would like to purchase. Have children make their selections from the flavors you provide and remind them to say "please" and "thank you" when being served. After each child "pays" you for the ice cream treat, set a cookie on a napkin and then place a small scoop of ice cream on top of that cookie. Hand the child a second cookie to place on top of the ice cream. The child can finish making the sandwich by squeezing the layers together before eating it. For an added treat, dip the second cookie in melted chocolate before giving it to the child. Play the music again while moving to your next customer. What a delicious way to end a play day at the "park."

Community Connections

To learn more about the specialized jobs for operating a park facility, invite a city recreation worker, swimming coach, lifeguard, or park maintenance worker to talk to the children. Additional information about inviting visitors into the classroom is provided on page 6.

Material

- Picture book as listed

Kindergarten Corner: Tai Chi

It is also common for people to use public parks for exercise. Particularly in China, tai chi is performed by large groups of people. Tai chi (pronounced tie chee) was started many years ago. It is a slow movement activity that helps reduce stress and improves balance and agility. For example, pose with hands stretched out—one hand in front of the body and one in back. Stretch your legs in a lunge position with the back foot turned to the side. This pose is held for a short time until another pose is chosen. Be sure your movements are slow and controlled. Refer to a book on Tai chi, such as *Step-by-Step Tai Chi* by Master Lam Kam Chuen (Fireside, 1994) or make up your own poses and movements as you perform tai chi together as a class on the playground.

File Folder Game: All Around the Park

Materials

- 2 water-soluble markers in different colors
- Colorful card stock
- Colorful copier paper
- Colorful file folder
- Die
- Laminating material
- Markers
- Scissors and glue
- Zippered plastic bag

Getting Ready

1. Make one copy of this page and the game board on pages 63 and 64 on colorful copier paper. Using colorful card stock, make one copy of the game cards on page 65. Laminate the game cards for durability before cutting them out. Cut out the "To Play" instruction box below.

2. Open the folder and orient it so that the tab is on the right. Write the title "All Around the Park" on the tab to identify the game. If desired, add additional color to the game board scene. Trim around the game board scene pieces as needed. Glue the two scene pieces to the file folder so that the borders meet at the center of the fold, making a continuous path through the park.

3. Close the folder and glue the "To Play" instruction box on the front panel.

4. Laminate the entire file folder for durability. Trim around the edges.

5. Store the game cards and the markers in a zippered plastic bag. Write the title of the game on a piece of paper and tape it to the front of the bag.

To Play

1. Each player draws a game card and chooses a different color of marker.

2. Player #1 rolls the die. Starting on the star and moving toward the place pictured on the game card, that player draws a line on the path across the same number of spaces as shown on the die.

3. Player #2 takes a turn and rolls the die. Starting on the star, that player also moves down the path in the same manner.

4. When a player lands on the place pictured on the card, the player keeps the game card, returns to the star, and draws a new card.

5. It may take more than one turn to "walk" to the place shown on a game card. If so, the player resumes drawing the line from the spot where it was stopped on the last turn.

6. The first player to visit three places in the park wins the game.

Having a Good Lunch

Materials

- 4 large sheets of brown craft paper
- Card stock and scissors
- Masking tape
- Music CD and player
- Yarn and hole punch

Getting Ready

- Make several copies of page 73 on card stock. Cut out the foods and follow the directions in the relay activity below to make food necklaces.
- Tape the four large sheets of brown craft paper to the floor, far enough apart so that children may easily move between them. These will be the "lunch bags."

Discuss with children the importance of eating balanced meals. Show children the lunch foods on page 73. Tell them that in order to pack a good lunch, they need one of each of these food items. Choose four children to be "lunch packers" and assign one of the craft paper "lunch bags" to each. Direct the other children to wear the lunch food necklaces you have prepared. Put on some playful music and let children dance. Periodically stop the music and have the lunch packers individually choose one food item (worn by a child) to "pack" in their lunches. Continue the game by playing the music and stopping it randomly so that children can pack more food items into each bag. Remind the "food items" in the bags to sit and not fall out of the bags where they might be squashed. After the fifth round of selecting food, there should be a sandwich, milk, fruit, vegetable, and cookie in each bag. Play the game again as time and interest allow.

Hall Pass Relay Game

Materials

- 4 bean bags
- 4 index cards
- Hole punch
- Marker
- Masking tape
- Yarn and scissors

Getting Ready: Write the words "hall pass" on four index cards. Punch a hole in each card, thread one end of a 2 ft. (61 cm) length of yarn through the hole, and knot the ends to create a necklace. Optional: Students may hold the word cards instead of wearing necklaces. Place one long piece of masking tape on the floor to make a "start" line on one side of the room and a second piece of tape to create a "turn-around" line on the other side. Finally, make a tape trail on the floor that zigzags across the room from the start line to the second line. Repeat this procedure to make four different trails.

How to Play: Divide the class into four teams. Have each team line up at the start line. Tell children that in order to leave the classroom to get a drink of water or use the bathroom, they must have a "hall pass." Each of the taped paths is a "hall." The first player for each team wears the hall pass necklace (or holds it) and balances the beanbag on her head. On your signal, all of the first players of the teams walk carefully and quickly along the zigzagged paths to the other side of the room and then back again, trying to keep the beanbags on their heads. The second players in line then take the hall pass necklaces and the beanbags and make their way down and back the hall paths. Play continues until all members of one team finish the relay to win the game.

Dramatic Play Center: My Little School

Materials

- Blocks
- Books, paper, pencils, and write-on and wipe-off materials
- Large or small boxes
- Small, plastic people and doll-house furniture
- Toy buses and cars

Whether you have a large open space or a very small space that can be converted into a learning center, it is easy to use boxes to encourage imaginative play. In large open spaces, set up the area with appliance boxes placed on their sides. If there is not enough space to use large boxes, you may consider gathering small boxes and creating an imaginary schoolroom using doll-house furniture or other items you can find in the toy box. Do the same when creating spaces that represent the gym, lunchroom, library, and other areas in your pretend school. Supply toy buses and cars for "transportation" to and from school. Additional materials to gather for the play center may include books, paper, pencils, and write-on and wipe-off materials. Watch what happens when young learners take over the play center!

Community Connections

If your children are in kindergarten, perhaps the first-grade teacher could visit your classroom and answer questions students may have about that grade. It may also be possible for your students to visit a first-grade classroom and find out what it looks like.

Kindergarten Corner: School Around the World

Material

- Picture book as listed

All over the world, children attend school. However, not all classrooms look the same. Read aloud *School Days Around the World* by Catherine Chambers (Dorling Kindersley Limited, 2007) and discuss similarities and differences among schools worldwide.

File Folder Game: Stuff the Bus ✳

Materials

- Colorful file folder
- Craft knife
- Markers
- Scissors
- Zippered plastic bags

Getting Ready

General directions: Using colorful card stock, make one copy of this page and two copies of page 74. Cut out each bus and also cut out the inside of each window. Open the folder and orient it so that the tab is on the right. Write the title "Stuff the Bus" on the tab to identify the game. Affix two buses to each inside panel of the file folder by gluing only the front, back, and bottom edge of each bus. After closing the folder, cut out the "To Play" instruction box below and glue it to the front panel.

Laminate the prepared folder and then use a craft knife to make a slit along the roof line of each bus to create a pocket. Next, carefully cut around each window so that the children game pieces (see below) can be slipped into the bus and be seen through the windows.

Game A—Color matching game: Make one copy of page 75 on card stock. Color the T-shirts of the children game pieces as follows: four red, four green, four yellow, and four blue. Color the other clothing as desired. Cut out the children and laminate them for durability. Store the game pieces in a zippered plastic bag and staple it to the outside panel of the prepared file folder.

Game B—Shape matching game: Make one copy of page 75 on card stock. Draw shapes on the T-shirts of the children game pieces as follows: a circle on four, a triangle on four, a square on four, and a rectangle on four. Color the clothing as desired. Cut out the children game pieces and laminate them for durability. Store the game pieces in a zippered plastic bag and staple it to the outside panel of the prepared file folder.

If the class is sorting the colors of T-shirts, use water-soluble markers to identify the categories. Draw a matching color outline—red, green, yellow, or blue—around each bus before setting the materials in the learning center.

If the class is sorting the geometric shapes shown on T-shirts into groups, label the buses accordingly to identify the categories. Use a black water-soluble marker to draw matching shapes—circles, triangles, squares, or rectangles—on each bus before playing the game.

✂

To Play

1. Take the game pieces out of the bag.
2. **Game A:** Match the color of the T-shirt to the color outline of the bus. Slide each game piece into the correct bus.
3. **Game B:** Match the shape on each T-shirt to the shape drawn on the side of the bus. Slide each game piece into the correct bus.

School Bus *(Refer to directions on page 5 and page 166.)*

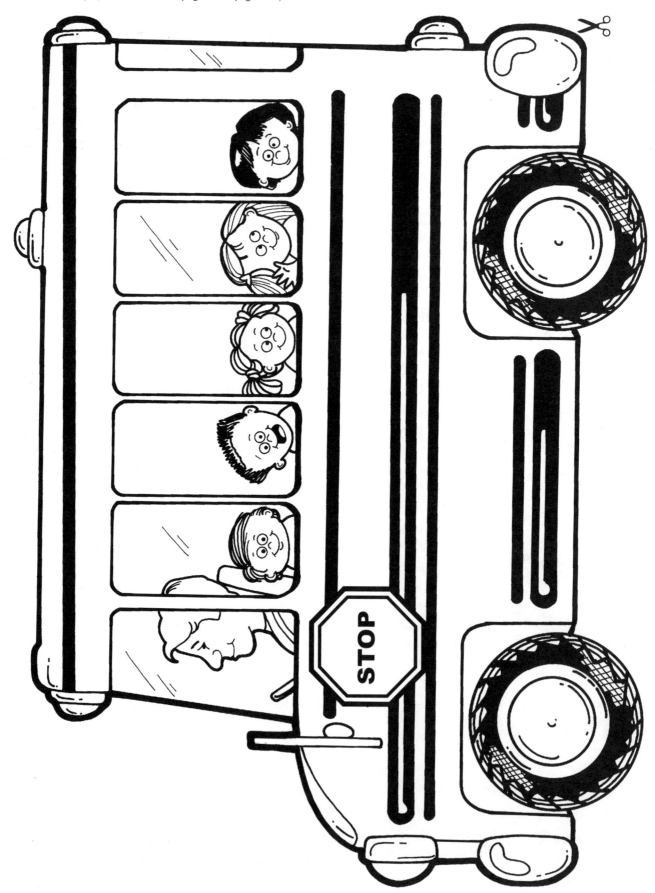

Planning the Day Clipboard *(Refer to directions on page 66.)*

Planning the Day Activity Cards *(Refer to directions on page 66.)*

 eat lunch

 wash hands

 play outside

 play a game

 build with blocks

 read a book

 play with sand

 sing a song

 paint a picture

 write my name

 dance to music

 rest quietly

 count things

 dress up and pretend

Having a Good Lunch Food Patterns *(Refer to directions on page 67.)*

Stuff the Bus Patterns *(Refer to directions on page 69.)*

74

Stuff the Bus Children Game Pieces
(Refer to directions on page 69.)

The Library

Materials

- Crayons and glue
- Picture books as listed
- Reference books such as those about outer space, animals, etc.
- Your favorite book

Getting Ready

- Make a copy of the *At the Library* booklet on pages 81 and 82 and cut an additional half sheet of copier paper for each child. Then, cut out the pages, assemble the booklet, and include a blank page at the back.
- For each child, set the copy of the library card aside to complete for page 3 of the booklet.

At the Library ✳

The library is a place where anyone can go to borrow books. Discuss that some libraries also keep movies, magazines, newspapers, and recorded music in their collections, as well as offer some special services, such as story hour and the use of computers for research and playing educational games. Explain that children can learn something about most topics at the library. Some neighborhoods have great big libraries while other neighborhoods have to wait for a bookmobile (a library on wheels) to bring books to them. Read aloud *My Librarian Is a Camel: How Books Are Brought to Children Around the World* by Margriet Ruurs (Boyds Mills Press, 2005) to learn about the ways children all over the world have access to books.

Talk about librarians—people who work at the library. Besides helping people find books or search for answers to questions, they also recommend books for them to read. Share *The Boy Who Was Raised by Librarians* by Carla Morris (Peachtree, 2007) or *Tomás and the Library Lady* by Pat Mora (Knopf, 1997) to illustrate one way librarians influence the lives of young children. Point out that the author of *Tomás and the Library Lady* is actually the little boy in the story. Read Mr. Mora's biography to children and highlight all the things he has been able to accomplish because someone encouraged his love of books.

Not everyone likes to read the same kind of stories. That is the reason why there are so many different kinds of books in a library—some books tell imaginary stories while other books tell about people's lives, animals, places, or things. Show the class your favorite book and explain why you enjoyed reading it. You may also wish to give a brief synopsis of the book. After the discussion, invite children to spend time in the classroom library center, exploring books. Have each child select one favorite book and bring it to circle time to share with the class. When presenting their selections, have children individually sit in a chair in front of the class and "read" the book by showing and telling about the pictures contained in it.

Finally, wrap up the lesson by giving each child the booklet *At the Library*. Color and complete booklet pages 2 and 3 as directed on pattern pages 81 and 82. On the blank booklet page 4, have the child draw a picture of a favorite book and in the remaining space on the page, "write" the book's title and a sentence to explain why it is a favorite.

Taking Care of Books

Materials

- 2 or 3 well-worn picture books
- Bucket of water
- Towel
- Used paperback chapter book

Getting Ready

- Tear several pages out of one of the picture books.

During story hour, read the picture book that has had some pages removed. Make a dramatic production (i.e., look under the book, shake it upside down, and so on) to illustrate that something is missing. See if children can tell you what is wrong with the book. Explain to them that the pages are missing because they were torn out. Therefore, it is not possible to enjoy this story ever again. Continue the discussion by talking about why it is important to know how to handle books carefully. Show children how to turn a book's pages at the corner and how to stack books on the shelf properly. Demonstrate other destructive ways of handling a book, like touching it with dirty hands, coloring on it, bending its covers backwards until the spine breaks, and so on.

People's actions are not the only things that destroy books. Books that are exposed to water or excessive sunlight can also be ruined. Ask children what they think will happen if you drop a book into water. After fielding their ideas, take an old paperback book and immerse it in a bucket of water. Pull the book out of the water and lay it on a towel. Allow children to check on the book throughout the day and observe what happens to the pages as they air dry.

Book Club Talk

Materials

- 5 copies of a popular picture book
- Crackers and juice
- Fancy china plates and teacups (or play dishes)
- Paper napkins

Gather a small group of children and have them sit around a table. Give each child a napkin and demonstrate placing a napkin on the lap. Serve your small group some juice in teacups and crackers on plates. Offer each child a copy of the book you are going to read and remind everyone to be careful not to spill any juice on a book or touch it with cracker-crumbed fingers.

Once the group is settled, have all children open up their books. Point out where to find the author's and illustrator's names, the book title, and copyright and other information, such as where the book was published, how the pictures were created, and so on. Turn to the dedication page and explain the tradition of dedicating books. Have children turn to the first page of the story and look at the pictures to determine what they think the words might say. Begin reading the book together, pausing occasionally to talk about the relationship between the pictures and the text. (Sometimes there is more of the story told in the pictures than with words.) When you have finished reading the book to the group, ask questions about the story. Let the book club participants take turns telling you about their favorite parts of the story and whether or not they would recommend the book to a friend as everyone finishes the juice and crackers.

Sorting Books ✳

Materials

- Pencil
- Picture storybooks and other types of books
- Tape and paper

Gather a small collection of books and have children help you sort them into groups. You might stack picture storybooks in one pile and nonfiction books in another. Alternatively, you might consider having children sort the books by size. Once all books have been sorted, extend the lesson by attaching a number to each book within a group. For example, start with a picture storybook and write the numeral 1 on a piece of paper. Tape that number to the spine of the book. Repeat the process with the other picture storybooks in the group. When all of the books have been labeled, let children arrange them in numerical order on a bookshelf in the dramatic play center.

Shhhh, Please! ✳

Materials

- Card stock, tape, and ruler
- Markers and scissors
- Musical instruments

Getting Ready

- Copy the librarian on page 82 onto card stock. Color, cut out, and tape the figure to a ruler.

Choose one child to be the "librarian." Have the librarian sit in front of the other children, holding the librarian cutout figure behind her back. Sing the song, inserting the child's name where indicated. While singing, let children play their musical instruments until they hear the warning from the librarian, who pops out from behind the child's back. Repeat the game until everyone in the class gets to be the librarian.

At the Library

(Sing to the tune of "Pop Goes the Weasel")

When we visit our library,
We sometimes make some noise.
Up pops, [child's name], the librarian,
"Shhhh, please, girls and boys!"

Dramatic Play Center: Our Library

Materials

- Audio books, CD or tape players, and headphones
- Book lights
- Books
- Index cards and pencils
- Large pillows, small chairs, and table
- Reading glasses frames (without lenses)

If you already have a bookshelf loaded with wonderful picture books, consider adding a few furnishings nearby to change the area into a "library." Begin by setting up a small table or desk for the librarian to use. Make a library card for each child on an index card or use the pattern on page 82 and store the cards in a file box. For your author's corner, display any stories that the children have written.

Encourage children to use their library cards, check out books and audiotapes, and cozy up on large pillows with their good books. A child may enjoy "reading" a story with a pair of reading glasses or a book light. Let children take turns being the librarian who presents "story hour" for the class. Optional: Provide supplies for making bookmarks for children to take home.

Community Connections

Invite one or more of the following people to visit your classroom: children's librarian, library aide, book illustrator, or author. Additional information about inviting visitors is provided on page 6. As a follow-up activity, make arrangements to visit a public library for a behind-the-scenes tour and stay for story hour.

Kindergarten Corner: Give This Book a Title

Materials

- Favorite picture books

During group time, show children an assortment of familiar books. Point out that the title of a book usually gives a clue about the story. Have each child pick out a favorite book. Choose one or two of the selected books and read them aloud to the class. When you are finished, invite children to think of other possible titles for the books. Continue the activity for several days until all of the children's selections have been read and discussed.

Bookmobile *(Refer to directions on page 5 and page 166.)*

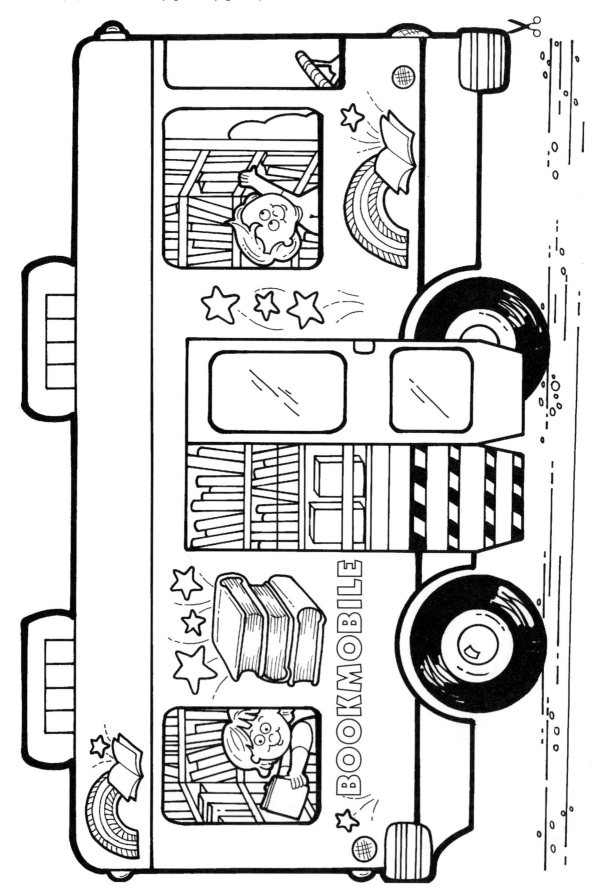

To the teacher: Make one copy of the booklet (pages 81 and 82) for each child. Cut out each page along the dashed lines. On page 2, have the child draw a book cover in the empty box. *(To assemble the booklet, refer to page 76 for more directions.)*

At the Library

Name:

Big books, little books, and
medium ones, too,
All are at the library waiting for you.

2

To the teacher: Have the child glue the completed library card in the box on page 3.

Glue library card here.

You can borrow books. It's really not hard.
All you are going to need is a library card.

3

To the teacher: To make the library card, have the child sign it, draw a self-portrait in the box, and cut it out along the dashed lines.

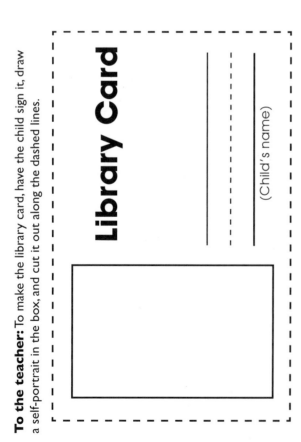

Library Card

(Child's name)

Librarian
(Refer to directions on page 78.)

The Grocery Store

Materials

• Picture books as listed
• Tall paper grocery bag
• Various food items

Getting Ready

• Make a copy of the *At the Grocery Store* booklet on pages 88 and 89 for each child. Collate and staple the pages after they have been completed.

Materials

• Aprons and plastic food server gloves
• Clipboard, pencil, and sticky-back notepaper
• Scale
• Table
• Various fruits and vegetables

At the Grocery Store

What can you buy at a grocery store? Talk about various kinds of food and other household items for sale at grocery stores. To purchase food or other items, they must be brought to the checkout counter to be paid for and then packed in bags to take home. Read aloud *To Market, To Market* by Anne Miranda (Voyager, 2001) or *What's in Grandma's Grocery Bag?* by Hui-Mei Pan (Star Bright Books, 2004). Let children try to recall the events of the story and name the things that were brought home from the store.

While children sit in a circle, set a few food items on the floor in front of them. Talk about each one before placing it in the paper grocery bag. When all of the selected foods are packed, challenge the children to recall what is in the bag without peeking inside it.

Wrap up the activity by giving each child a copy of the booklet *At the Grocery Store*. Follow the directions on pages 88 and 89 for completing the pages. Later, share the booklets during circle time.

What's in the Produce Department?

The produce manager at a grocery store must take care of the fresh fruits and vegetables that are for sale. Place an assortment of fruits and vegetables in a bowl. Have children don aprons and wear plastic gloves while they weigh each piece of produce on a small scale. Items that weigh more than 1 pound (454 grams) should be placed on one end of the table and those items that weigh less than 1 pound (454 grams) should be placed at the other end. The criteria for the sorting task could also be color, kind of food, or shape.

Alternatively, have children arrange the fruits and vegetables in order from lightest to heaviest. After they weigh each piece of produce, record its weight on a piece of sticky-back notepaper and then stick the note to the table. Set the food item near its recorded weight. It works well to use a clipboard to hold the sticky-backed notes. Be sure to rearrange the order of the produce as necessary until the project is finished.

After everyone has had an opportunity to weigh and sort produce, wash the foods (and hands) thoroughly and allow children to use plastic knives to cut up the fruits and vegetables for snack. (NOTE: Follow your school's guidelines for serving foods in the classroom.) Practice cutting things in half, then in half again until all pieces are bite sized. Have children talk about the colors, seeds, and other interesting details that they notice. Does their produce have a skin that can be eaten? Is it heavy for its size? During the discussion about each food, write down one descriptive word from each child on a piece of paper. Then, when that food is served, use the words to describe it. For example, you might announce that everyone will now be eating a "bumpy, orange, triangular-shaped snack."

Materials

- Aprons
- Cheese slices
- Containers of purchased side dishes (fruit salad, lettuce salad, etc.)
- Deli meats
- Lettuce and tomato slices
- Paper hat or hair nets
- Plastic food server gloves
- Plastic knives and forks
- Plastic wrap or sandwich bags
- Sandwich bread slices
- Small deli containers

Deli Department: Order to Go

After washing their hands thoroughly, children can don paper hats, plastic gloves, and aprons to be ready for work in the "deli department." (NOTE: Follow your school's guidelines for serving foods in the classroom.) Set up a few tables and label one of them as the "deli counter." Demonstrate how to assemble simple deli sandwiches by stacking meat, cheeses, and vegetables onto sandwich bread slices. Talk about the sequence in which the items are placed. Use words like *first*, *middle*, and *last*. Have children take turns being a worker or a customer at the deli counter. After a customer orders, the deli worker should make the sandwich, cut it into fourths, and then wrap it in plastic wrap or place it in a plastic bag. Include a serving of salad in a small container with the sandwich. Switch roles, so that all children get a chance to work and snack at your grocery deli.

Materials

- Baking tray
- Cardboard cut into simple shapes
- Disposable cake decorating bags
- Glitter or confetti (optional)
- Mixing bowl, spoon, and plastic knives
- Scissors
- Shaving cream
- Tempera paints
- Twist ties
- White glue

Bakery Department: Let's Decorate!

Getting Ready: Cut several large shapes out of cardboard. Prepare glue "frosting" by mixing $1/3$ cup (78 mL) of white glue with 2 cups (470 mL) of shaving cream. The consistency should be that of meringue. Add more shaving cream if the mixture is flat and not fluffy. Add color by mixing spoonfuls of tempera paint into the frosting. Repeat to make additional colors. (Glitter can also be added to the mixture if desired.) Spoon the glue frosting into disposable decorator bags and seal the open ends with twist ties. (Use squeeze bottles if managing the decorator tips is too difficult.)

Activity: The bakery department at a grocery store makes fresh baked goods every day. The workers bake many tasty things: breads, cookies, special desserts, and birthday and wedding cakes. Read *Jake Baked the Cake* by B.G. Hennessy (Puffin, 1992) and talk about the steps taken to produce a beautiful cake. Then, have some creative fun by decorating "cake tops" in the classroom. Let each child choose a cardboard shape. Snip off the ends of the decorator bags with a pair of scissors. Squeeze the bags gently to create piped frosting. Let children make decorative designs or write their names on the cake tops. It is also possible to spread the glue frosting with a plastic knife and sprinkle it with glitter or confetti. (The glue frosting will dry as puffy 3-D frosting.)

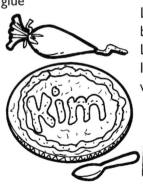

Bag It!

Materials

- Assorted empty food boxes, canned goods, and snack food items
- Paper grocery bags (easier to use than plastic bags) in various sizes

After purchasing various kinds of foods at a grocery store, talk about how people bring the items home. Learning how to pack different foods in grocery bags is actually a lot of fun. Set the foods on one table and the paper bags on a different table. After demonstrating how big items fit best in big bags and little items fit best in little bags, allow children to experiment with packing the food items in paper grocery bags. Encourage children to add more items to a bag if there is space for them. Play other bagging games by having children sort food items and bag them according to a specified attribute, such as color.

What Happens to "Bad" Food?

Materials

- Assorted food products in packages with freshness or "sell by" dates stamped on them
- Clear plastic wrap
- Digital camera
- Foil pans
- Heavy packing tape
- Magnifying glasses
- Paper and pencil
- Small pieces of fruit, bread (without preservatives), and vegetables

Show the class the various food items. Talk with children about the fact that grocery stores try to provide the very best foods to their customers. Explain that sometimes food gets old before it can be sold and then it must be discarded. Spoiled food can make a person very sick if eaten. To prevent this from happening, some products have dates stamped on them. Hold up the different products you have collected and point out the freshness dates.

To investigate what happens to food when it spoils, gather small pieces of fruit, vegetables, and bread (without preservatives). Lightly rub the piece of bread across a surface. Place each food sample in a separate foil pan. Take a photo of the food with a digital camera. Cover the pans with clear plastic wrap and secure the wrap in place with heavy packing tape. Have children predict what they think will happen to each food sample over time. Record their predictions on paper and tape them to the corresponding pans. Place the pans on a warm windowsill or tabletop where they will not be disturbed by little hands. In a couple of days, show children the pans and observe any changes in the foods. (CAUTION: Do not smell the food samples or remove the plastic wrap from the containers.) Continue the investigation over the next few weeks. Each time, compare the rotting samples to the digital photos. Note which foods changed a lot and if there were any that did not change at all. Discard the foil pans when finished.

Dramatic Play Center: Our Food Mart

Materials

- Assortment of empty food containers and plastic food items
- Grocery bags, cash register, and play money
- Paper and markers

Set up a small grocery store in the play center. Provide a cash register, play money, and grocery bags at a checkout counter. Fill shelves with plastic food items, canned goods, empty cereal and cracker boxes, and empty (clean) plastic food tubs. Provide shopping baskets and play money for shoppers. Children can make signs for the sale items. Then, open your food mart for business.

Reusable Shopping Bags

Materials

- Cloth, paper, and plastic grocery bags
- Craft materials for decorating the cloth bags
- Large metal clips, two chairs, and canned food

Discuss with children that using paper and plastic grocery bags can be very wasteful. To make paper bags, trees must be cut down. Some kinds of plastic bags are made from a substance that does not decay. That means they stay in our trash cans and landfills unless they are recycled.

Continue the lesson by setting up an experiment for children to complete. Have them test the strength of three kinds of grocery bags—paper, plastic, and cloth—by dropping a heavy can of food into each one. To conduct the experiment, place two chairs a short distance apart. Using large metal clips, hang an open paper bag between the two chairs. Hold the can a distance above the bag and then drop it into the bag. Repeat the test several times until the bag tears or breaks. Continue the investigation with the plastic bag and then the cloth bag. During group time, talk about the results and have children determine which bag was the strongest.

Finally, let children individually decorate cloth shopping bags. Solicit parent donations of cloth bags or perhaps the owner of your local grocery store would be willing to donate bags or discount the cost of purchasing them. Provide children with craft paints or other craft materials to use.

Community Connections

Arrange for an excursion to a local grocery store. While most children are familiar with that business, a behind-the-scenes look at the inner workings of the store would be a new experience. Read aloud *Do the Doors Open by Magic? And Other Supermarket Questions* by Catherine Ripley (Owl Books, 1995) and talk about the interesting things people might see at a grocery store.

Before leaving on your field trip, plan the menu for a simple snack with the class and then make a shopping list for the needed items.

Take along your newly decorated shopping bags and have children look for certain things. If you have enough parent supervision, make copies of pictures of several different food items found in a grocery store (e.g., the front panel of a cereal box). Divide the class into small groups and send them off to find the specified items.

Kindergarten Corner: How Much for That?

Materials

- Assorted items to purchase
- Paper and markers
- Play money
- Shelves

Gather an assortment of small trinkets and toys and sort them into groups. Label each shelf with a price. For example, everything on the top shelf costs 5¢ each, on the second shelf things cost 10¢ each, and so on. Place the items on the corresponding shelves. Give each shopper play money and let children "purchase" items in the classroom store.

Delivery Truck *(Refer to directions on page 5 and page 166.)*

To the teacher: Make one copy of the booklet (pages 88 and 89) for each child. Cut out each page along the dashed lines. On page 2, have the child clip a picture of a favorite treat from a grocery store flier and glue it on the grocery cart.

2

I see many good things to eat.

If I were shopping,

I'd put _____

in my cart for a treat.

At the Grocery Store

EGGS

BREAD

Peaches

MILK

FUDGE

COOKIES

Name:

To the teacher: On page 3, have the child draw and color an apple above the head shown. On page 4, have the child clip pictures of foods from grocery store fliers and glue them on the bag.

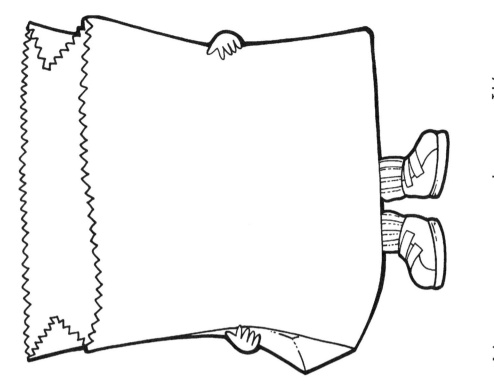

4

Now, we are done. It's time to go. What's in your bag? I'd like to know.

3

I have cereal, crackers, juice, and bread. Look, I'm balancing this apple on my head!

Materials

- Card stock
- Crayons
- Firefighter costume
- Paper, scissors, and stapler

Getting Ready

- Using card stock, make three copies of the fire pattern on page 98. Color each fire and cut it out.
- Using card stock, make four or five copies of the fire truck on page 94 and cut out along the solid line. Write a fire safety rule on the back of each truck.
- Make a copy of the fire truck on page 94 for each child. Write "My Fire Safety Book" on the fire truck. Stack four sheets of paper behind each truck and staple the booklet along the left edge. Cut through all thicknesses around the fire truck to make the shaped booklet.

Materials

- Clothespins
- Craft paper
- Firefighter hats
- Paintbrushes
- Spray bottles filled with water
- Tempera paints

The Fire Station

Where's the Fire?

The fire station is a busy place. At any time during the day or night, people may call there for help. Whether the call is for a rescue or to put out a fire, firefighters are always ready. Read aloud *Fire Fighter Piggy Wiggy* by Christyan and Diane Fox (Handprint, 2001) or another book about the kinds of jobs that firefighters will do if needed.

When someone calls 9-1-1 needing the help of a firefighter, the call goes to a dispatcher. The dispatcher relays the message to the fire station, telling the firefighters the location of the fire and how to get there. Have a child dress up in a firefighter's costume (or just wear the hat) and stand briefly outside the classroom door, just until the alarm is sounded. Choose a child to be the "dispatcher." The dispatcher hides three "fires" around the room. Then, make a siren noise (the other children can help you with this). When the firefighter re-enters the room, give instructions on how to find the first fire. You might say, for example, "Go around the table and look behind the book." When the three fires are "extinguished," choose two new children to be the dispatcher and firefighter.

Once everyone has had an opportunity to play the game, talk about the things that we can do to prevent fires and how we can stay safe during a fire. Set the fire truck cards faceup in front of the children. Choose one child to select a card and "read" the fire safety rule on the back. To reinforce what has been discussed, give each child a prepared booklet. Have children dictate or "write" fire safety rules on the pages and then illustrate them as desired.

Art: Paint and Douse

What happens when water is sprayed on wet paint? To let children find out the result, first have them paint their sheets of craft paper with the tempera paints. Encourage them to use lots of colorful paint. When the paintings are complete, clip each one to a fence or clothesline outside. Have children don firefighter hats and douse their paintings with water. Watch what happens to the paint as it gets soaked.

Beat the Clock!

Materials

- Assorted objects for an obstacle course (cones, boxes, jump ropes, hula hoops, floor mats, etc.)
- Colorful card stock
- Dowel
- Laminating material
- Spray bottles filled with water
- Stopwatch

Getting Ready: Create a short obstacle course where children perform three or four different activities in a row as they move from one side of a large outdoor play area to the other side. For example, children can hop around four cones, jump through a series of hula hoops, walk along a rope (as if it were a tightrope), and crawl through a tunnel of boxes.

Using colorful card stock, make several copies of the fire pattern on page 98. Color and cut out the pictures as desired (you may wish to trim off the wood in the picture) and then laminate them. Tape a fire picture to a dowel. At the end of the obstacle course, stick one end of the dowel into the ground.

To Play: Firefighters always need to move quickly. Tell children they are going to play a game called Beat the Clock. Explain that you will watch the clock to see how fast they can line up at the door. Then, give the signal for them to move. Announce the number of seconds it took to line up. Repeat the activity to see if they can do the task faster the second time to "beat the clock."

Demonstrate the obstacle course and explain this version of Beat the Clock. Tell children that they are firefighters on their way to a "fire." Point out the obstacles in their way and that they must run around, jump over, and crawl through them to reach the fire. Give children spray bottles to carry as they run through the obstacle course. When they reach the fire, they can use their spray bottles to "put the fire out" by squirting it with water.

I'm a Firefighter

I'm a tiny firefighter as you can see; (Hold hands as though looking through binoculars.)

Whenever there is fire trouble, people call me. (Point to self.)

I race to the fire as fast as can be. (Run in place and roll arms.)

This is what you'll hear because I am ready. (Hold hand to ear.)

Ding—clank, clank, clank, and whoosh! (Tap top of head with an open palm, move hands overhead as climbing a ladder, and squat while lowering hands. Hold hose in hands and pretend to spray water from one side to the other.)

Ding—clank, clank, clank, and whoosh! (Repeat actions.)

Note: Use a high voice for the tiny firefighter, a regular voice for the medium-sized firefighter, and a low voice for the great big firefighter.

Repeat the rhyme with other verses:

I'm a medium-sized firefighter as you can see ...

I'm a great big firefighter as you can see ...

Dramatic Play Center: Fire, Fire!

Materials

- Colorful card stock
- Desk, phone, and clipboard
- Firefighter hats and jackets
- Garden hose
- Hose keeper (for storing hose)
- Laminating material
- Sticky-tack adhesive
- Traffic cones and wagon

Getting Ready: Using colorful card stock, make several copies of the fire pattern on page 98. Color as desired, cut out (you may wish to trim off the wood in the picture), and laminate them. Place a small ball of Sticky-tack adhesive on the back of each one. Display the pictures around the room. Create a dispatch center with the desk, phone, and clipboard and place the hose, hose keeper, and traffic cones in the wagon.

Activity: Have children don the firefighter costumes and hit the road to put out fires that have been called into the dispatch center. Arrange the traffic cones to block the road and then use the hose to "squirt water" on the fire. When the fire is out, wind up the hose, put the traffic cones back into the wagon, and return to the fire station to wait for the next emergency.

Stomp Out Campfire Sparks

Materials

- Laminating material
- Masking tape
- Music CD and player

Getting Ready

- Using colorful card stock, make several copies of the fire pattern on page 98. Color, cut out, and laminate them for durability.

To reinforce the importance of being careful when near a campfire, set up this fun activity in a large open space. Scatter the pictures of fires around the play area and tape them to the floor. Play some lively music and have children move between the fires, stamping out "sparks" near each campfire before moving on. Give children suggestions on how to move from one fire to the next and indicate when to stomp on sparks. Ideas might include skipping between fires, walking backwards, hopping on one foot, jumping, and so on. Remind children that if they accidentally step on a fire cutout, they must sit at the edge of the playing area for a few minutes because it is important to stay away from fires. Then, welcome them back to play. Finally, when it is time to stop the activity, have children "pour water" on the campfires to put out the flames.

Kindergarten Corner: All in a Day's Work

Materials

- Large clock with a second hand
- Marker and paper

Explore the concept of time with the class. Show children the large clock. Point out the different hands and have children watch the second hand move for a minute or two. Explain that sometimes a minute seems like a long time and sometimes it seems to pass quickly, but a minute is always exactly the same amount of time. Ask children to give you examples of activities that take an hour, a minute, or a second. Then, to illustrate one minute, invite children to see if they can jump up and down for 60 seconds while you time them.

Make up a firefighter's schedule that has a different pretend activity on each hour. For example, 8:00—eat breakfast, 9:00—visit kindergarten to discuss fire safety rules, 10:00—check the fire extinguishers, and so on. For each activity, have a child help you move the hands of the clock to the appropriate hour. Be sure to include a firehouse emergency (such as stand up, spray an imaginary fire, and then sit back down) during group time.

File Folder Game: Hurry, Hurry, Fire, Fire!

Materials

- Card stock
- Clear packing tape
- Colorful copier paper
- Craft knife, scissors, and glue
- Die
- File folder
- Markers
- Small plastic box with lid

Getting Ready

1. Make one copy of this page and the game board on pages 95 and 96 on colorful copier paper. Using card stock, make one copy of the fire truck game markers and the "burning house" tabbed insert on page 97. Cut out the "To Play" instruction box and the file-folder name tags found on this page.

2. Open the folder and orient it so that the tab is on the right. Glue a name tag onto the tab to identify the game. Trim around the game board scene pieces as desired. Cut out the windows in the house. Glue the two scene pieces to the file folder so that the borders meet at the center of the fold, making one continuous path through the town. *Do not glue the lower right corner of the scene behind the house.* Close the folder and glue the "To Play" instruction box on the front panel.

3. Laminate the entire file folder for durability. Then, follow the directions on page 97 for assembling the burning house and making the game markers to complete the game.

4. Store the die and game markers in a small box; tape a name tag on the lid.

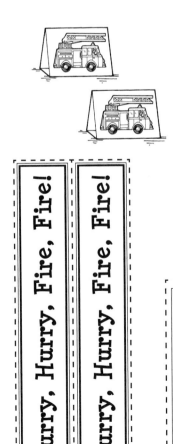

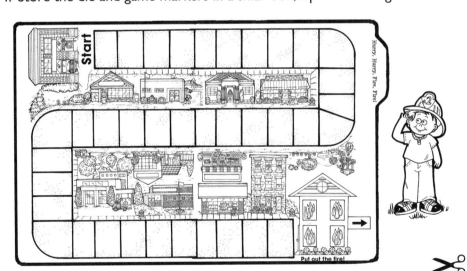

To Play

1. Place your fire truck on the fire station.
2. Take turns rolling the die and moving the same number of spaces as shown.
3. The first fire truck to make it to the house wins the game. Pull the tab to put out the fire!

Fire Truck *(Refer to directions on page 5 and page 166.)*

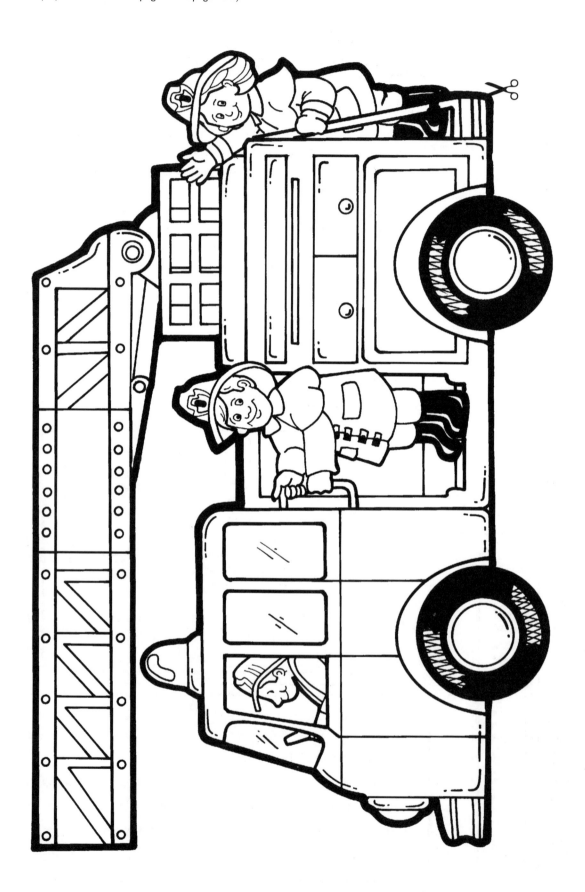

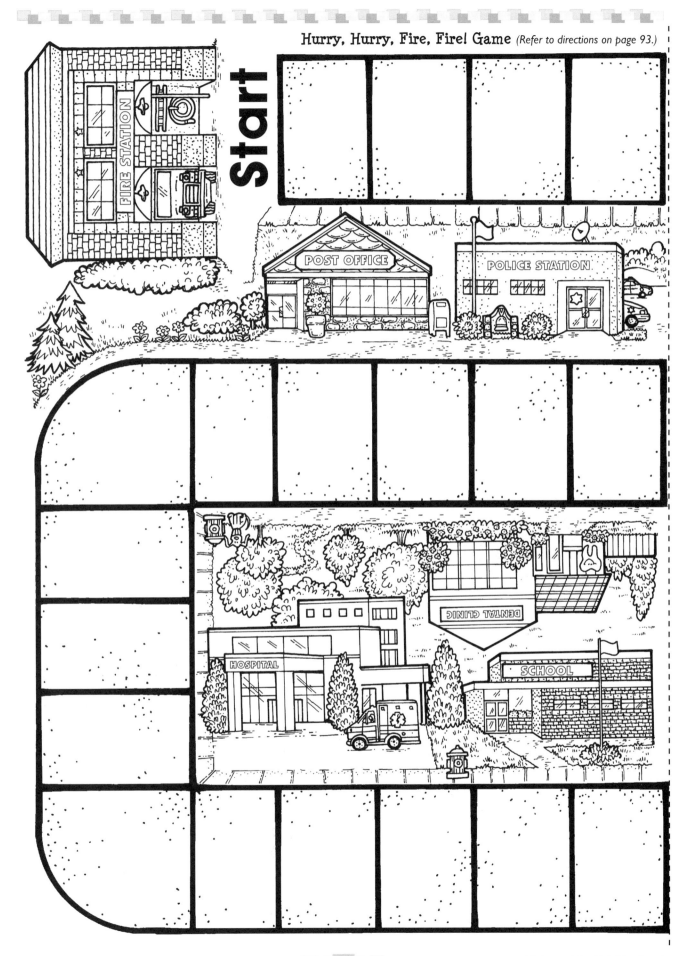

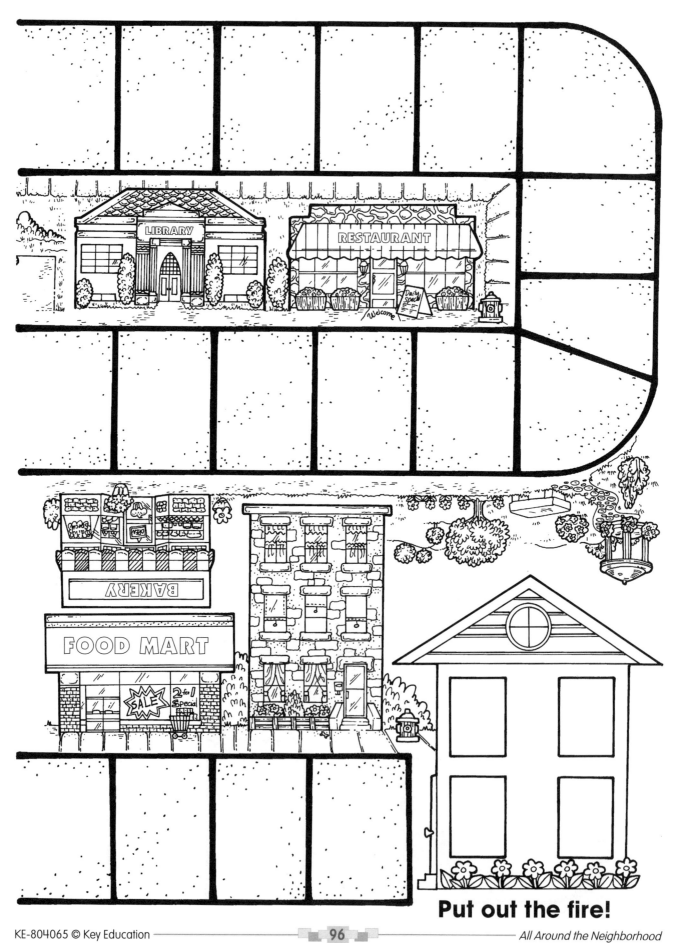

Put out the fire!

Tabbed Insert for Burning House and Fire Truck Game Markers *(Refer to directions on page 93.)*

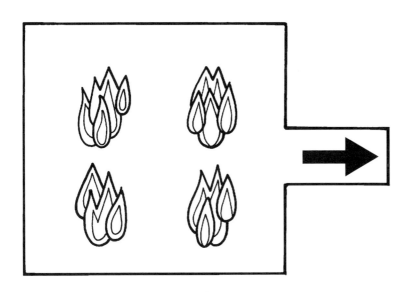

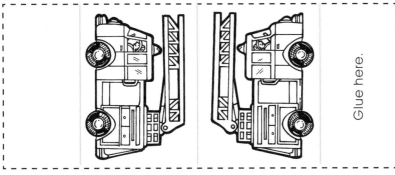

Glue here.

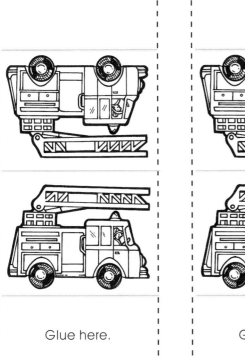

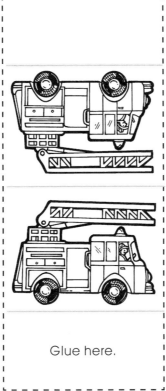

Glue here.   Glue here.

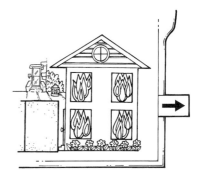

Burning House

Follow steps 1–3 on page 93.

4. Cut out the tabbed insert and laminate it for durability.

5. Use a craft knife to cut a 3" (76 mm) slit along the lower right corner of the game board to make a pocket behind the house.

6. Carefully cut around each window so that when the tabbed insert is slipped into the house pocket, the flames can be seen through the windows.

Game Markers

Follow steps 1–3 on page 93.

4. Color the three pairs of fire trucks, each pair a different color, and cut out the game markers along the dashed lines.

5. Laminate the markers for durability.

6. Fold each marker on the solid lines to make a triangular shape, overlapping the end panels. Glue as indicated.

Fire Pattern *(Refer to directions on pages 90–92.)*

The Police Station

Materials

- Large stuffed bear
- Picture books as listed
- Police officer costumes

Getting Ready

- Make a copy of the police officer on page 20. Cut out and glue the picture of the police officer in the middle of a sheet of paper. Across the top of the paper, write, "I can get help when I am lost." At the bottom, write, "My name: _____," "My parent's name: _____," and "My phone number: _____." Include a message to parents to explain the activity.
- Make a copy of this page for each child.
- Hide a large stuffed bear somewhere on the playground or in the classroom.

Looking for Mr. Bear

Police officers do many different kinds of jobs to help us stay safe. Explain that they respond to homes and businesses when there is an emergency. They patrol the roads to make sure drivers are following the traffic rules. They direct traffic to help school children cross the street safely. Read aloud *Policeman Small* by Lois Lenski (Random House, 2001), *The Police Cloud* by Christoph Niemann (Schwartz & Wade, 2007), *Police Cat* by Enid Hinkes (Albert Whitman & Co., 2005), or another book that highlights the events in a police officer's day.

Another way police officers help others is finding children who have become lost. Tell children that your good friend Mr. Bear was following you to school today, but he got lost on his way to the classroom, and you don't know where he is. You will need good police officers to find him. Have children don police hats, safety vests, and badges. Then, swear in each child as a new member of the "[your class's name] Police Force."

Give children clues about where they might find Mr. Bear, such as, "The last time I saw Mr. Bear, he was playing on the playground." Have children go out to the playground and look for Mr. Bear. Once the bear has been found, regroup in the classroom and talk about being lost. Have children act out what they would do if they suddenly became lost. Remind children that the most important thing to do if they become lost is to stop moving about. If they run all over, the person looking for them might not find them. If they are in a store or another public place, they can look for an employee, a security officer, or a mom with other kids to help them. Tell them that it is also important to know their full names, their parents' names, and their phone numbers so that the police officers can help them find their way home. (Send home the prepared sheet for parents to complete with their children.)

Repeat the activity by allowing a child to hide the bear out of sight of the other children and then tell the classmates a general clue to explain where Mr. Bear might be "lost." Continue the search-and-find activity as many times as needed until all children have had a chance to hide the bear and offer clues.

Rules to Keep Us Safe!

Materials

• Card stock
• Crayons and marker
• Picture book as listed

Getting Ready

• Using card stock, make 10 enlarged copies of the police officer on page 20.

Police officers help us obey rules. Talk about different kinds of rules: Some rules are important for keeping ourselves safe. Other rules are important for keeping others safe. Still others are important for helping people live safely and peacefully as neighbors. Read aloud *Officer Buckle and Gloria* by Peggy Rathmann (Putnam, 1995) and discuss the story, helping children draw conclusions about following safety rules.

Wrap up the activity by asking children to call out various safety rules and then write each one on the back of a police officer picture card. Put the rules that are for keeping ourselves safe in one pile, the rules for keeping others safe in a second pile, and the rules for living peacefully as neighbors in the third pile. Discuss the fact that rules are important for everyone, even though sometimes they may not be much fun. Distribute the rules picture cards so that children may finish illustrating them. Display the completed cards in a prominent place.

Meet the K-9 Unit

Materials

• Assorted objects for an obstacle course (cones, boxes, jump ropes, hula hoops, floor mats, etc.)
• Crackers for a small treat
• Newspaper and rubber bands
• Picture book as listed

Getting Ready

• Set up a short obstacle course that requires children to run on all fours through hoops and jump over obstacles.
• Roll up a small section of newspaper and secure it with a rubber band. Make one for each child. Place the rolled up newspapers at the end of the obstacle course.

Just like Officer Buckle (introduced in the above activity), many police officers use dogs to help them do their work. Dogs can assist police officers in finding things by smelling them or by helping catch people who have taken things that don't belong to them. Read aloud *Aero and Officer Mike: Police Partners* by Joan Plummer Russell (Boyds Mills Press, 2001) and talk about the interesting jobs that Aero the police dog does to help Officer Mike.

Have children work in teams of two members: one child as the "police officer" and the other as the "police dog." When the police officer gives the command to go, the police dog must run through the obstacle course on all fours, pick up a newspaper in its mouth, and return to the starting point. After the police dog drops the newspaper at the officer's feet, the officer gives the dog a treat. Switch roles and let the dog become the police officer and vice versa.

When everyone has had a chance to run through the obstacle course, switch partners' roles again and invite the police officers to "train" their dogs to do new tricks. This is done by the police officer performing an action (like jumping up in the air and clapping at the same time) while the police dog watches and then repeats the same action. (Optional: Each time the dog learns a new trick, it receives a training treat.) Once children have had a chance to "train" one another, invite each police officer and canine companion to perform their tricks for the whole class to see.

Fingerprints

Sometimes when someone has done something wrong, police officers will search for fingerprints. Have children look closely at their fingertips and try to see tiny ridges or patterns in their skin. Explain that every person has a set of fingerprints that is different from every other person in the whole world. When you touch things, you leave specks of dirt and oil on that surface. You cannot see the prints unless your fingers are really dirty, but police officers use special tools to see them.

Give each child a prepared copy of the *Whose Prints?* booklet. Have children touch the ink pad with their fingertips and then make fingerprints on the pages in the booklet as directed. To extend the lesson, encourage children to ask their classmates to make fingerprints on the backs of their booklet pages. Wrap up the activity by letting children use magnifying glasses to examine the collected prints to see how they differ.

Materials

- Magnifying glasses
- Pencils
- Stapler
- Washable ink pads in different colors

Getting Ready

- Prepare the booklet *Whose Prints?* for each child. Refer to pages 104 and 105.

Materials

- Cardboard box
- Colorful card stock
- Marker and tape
- Music CDs and player
- Paper plates
- Play money
- Sunglasses (optional)

Getting Ready

- To make a steering wheel for each child, cut a circle out of the center of a paper plate.
- Prepare some pretend traffic violation tickets on card stock to give to drivers.

Gross Motor Activity: Speed Zone

Take the class for a drive! Give each child a steering wheel and a pair of sunglasses to wear. Write the numerals 1 and 10 on separate pieces of card stock to make speed limit signs. Tape the two speed signs on the opposite sides of a cardboard box. Then, have children "start their engines" to drive around the room with their steering wheels. While they are moving, play music in two different tempos. (You may wish to clap along with the beat to emphasize the tempo as children drive.) If the beat is slow, show them the speed limit sign with number 1 on it and explain that traveling at speed 1 is very slow. Switch to music with a fast beat and show them the speed limit sign for 10. Explain that traveling at speed 10 is fast. Remind drivers that they will need to watch their speeds to make sure they are not moving too slowly or too quickly—otherwise, they will receive a ticket. If children are not sure at what speed to move by simply listening to the music, they can look at the speed sign. If anyone is speeding during a slow song or moving too slowly during a fast tempo, hand a ticket to that child. At the end of the activity, the tickets may be paid with play money.

Crossing Guard Game

Materials

- Masking tape
- Orange safety vest and badge
- Picture book as listed
- Red construction paper
- Ruler or dowel
- Whistles (one for each child)

Getting Ready

- Using masking tape, create a huge square on the floor.

A crossing guard is a special kind of worker who helps people cross the road safely. Read aloud the delightful book *Make Way for Ducklings* by Robert McCloskey (Viking Press, 2001) and talk about how Officer Michael helped the family of ducks make it safely across the busy road.

Choose one child to be the crossing guard. Have her put on the safety vest and a badge and stand in the middle of the square. Line up the remaining children around the edges of the square as if waiting to cross the street. When the crossing guard blows her whistle and signals "okay," allow children on one side of the square to cross to the other side. Once they are safely across, the crossing guard stops "oncoming traffic" so that children on another side of the square may cross the "street." Alternatively, incorporate different gross motor skills by having the crossing guard give everyone else specific directions on how to move when crossing the street (such as bear walk, walk backwards, skip, hop, etc.). Switch roles frequently so that each child gets to be the crossing guard.

Dramatic Play Center: Police Station

Materials

- Handheld voice communicators
- Orange safety vests
- Pads of paper (for "writing" tickets) and pencils
- Toy police cars
- Traffic cones

To encourage imaginative play about being a safety officer, gather various materials, such a traffic cones, safety vests, toy cars, paper and pencil, etc.

Community Connections

Invite special visitors to your classroom to share insights about their jobs. For example, you might wish to invite a police officer or school crossing guard to talk about safety rules. Additional information about inviting visitors is provided on page 6.

Kindergarten Corner: Who's a Stranger?

Material

- Picture book as listed

Who's a stranger? Most children will identify a stranger as an adult who looks "scary" to them. To help children begin to recognize the difference between "scary" and "stranger," invite several guests to visit your class at a designated time. Make sure to ask people who look very different from one another and include some people who are not known by the children. Discuss as a group which ones are strangers and which ones are not. Talk about the importance of staying safe and talking only to those people whom they know. Read aloud *Never Talk to Strangers* by Irma Joyce (Golden Books, 2009).

Police Car *(Refer to directions on page 5 and page 166.)*

103 *All Around the Neighborhood*

To the teacher: Make one copy of the booklet (pages 104 and 105) for each child. Cut out each page along the dashed lines. Collate the booklet pages and staple them together. On page 2, have the child make fingerprints all over the picture.

Name:

Whose Prints?

Whose fingerprints are on the floor?
Whose fingerprints are on the door?

To the teacher: On page 3, have the child make fingerprints all over the picture. On page 4, have the child make a single fingerprint on the magnifying glass.

Whose fingerprints are on the chair?
Whose fingerprints are everywhere?

MINE! That's who!
This is my fingerprint.

_____

I am _____.   4

The Post Office

Here Comes the Mail

Materials

• Picture books as listed

The U.S. Postal Service has no official motto or creed. However, one phrase has been used to describe the dedication of postal employees. Written by a man named Herodotus, the statement says "Neither snow, nor rain, nor heat, nor gloom of night . . ." will keep letter carriers from delivering the mail. Postal workers work hard every day. Some sort the mail, some drive postal trucks, and others deliver the mail on foot. Read aloud *Harvey Hare, Postman Extraordinaire* by Bernadette Watts (North-South, 1999). See if children can recall from the story all of the extraordinary steps that Harvey Hare took to ensure that the mail was delivered every day to the other animals. Another book to read aloud is *Mail Carriers* by Dee Ready (Bridgestone Books, 1998).

Sorting the Mail

Materials

• Card stock
• Envelopes and markers

Getting Ready

• Using card stock, make 26 copies of the postal truck on page 110. Write the letters of the alphabet, one on each truck.
• Gather an assortment of envelopes and label each one with an alphabet letter.

Display the fleet of postal trucks you have created. As the class sings the "ABC Song," have children help you arrange the trucks in alphabetical order. When completed, announce that the mail trucks are now ready to make deliveries but need to be "packed" with the correct envelopes. For example, the truck labeled with the letter *A* will deliver only those items that are addressed with the letter *A* and so on. Let children take turns sorting the letters by placing them below the correct mail trucks.

Weigh and Sort Packages

Materials

• Scale
• Sticky-back notepaper and pencils
• Various sizes of boxes containing objects of various weights, sealed with packing tape

Stack the boxes on the floor. On a table nearby, place a scale, a pad of sticky-back notepaper, and a pencil. Show children how to weigh a package and then write the number of pounds (or kilograms) on the paper. Attach the sticky note to the box and continue the same process for the other boxes. When all of the boxes have been weighed and marked, sort them by stacking those with similar weights together.

After children have had experiences with weighing and sorting packages, extend the activity by moving the materials to the dramatic play center (see page 109).

Collecting Stamps

Materials

- Canceled stamps
- Magnifying glasses
- Markers
- Paper
- Scissors and glue
- Stapler
- Tweezers
- Zippered plastic bags

Getting Ready

- Send home a letter requesting that each child bring in two or three canceled stamps clipped from used envelopes.
- Make a stamp-collecting booklet for each child. Copy the booklet cover on page 111. Stack two or three small sheets of blank paper behind each cover and staple them together.

Gather the canceled stamps that children have brought to school. Using tweezers, pick up one stamp and then allow children to look at it closely. Let them share their observations about its color, content, and size. Ask children if any of them noticed a number printed on the stamp. Explain that the number tells how much money the stamp costs. Talk about the current cost of first-class postage and let children know that whether they are sending a letter across the country or just next door, the cost is the same. However, letters being sent elsewhere in the world do cost more money to send. Carefully glue the stamp to one of the pages in a *My Stamp Collection* booklet. Let each child choose a stamp, pick it up with the tweezers, and then describe it to the class before showing it to classmates. Finally, have children glue the stamps in their stamp-collecting booklets. Set all of the materials in the writing center so that children may add other canceled stamps to their booklets as desired.

Extend the lesson by letting children be stamp designers. Give each child a sheet of the generic stamp shapes (page 111). Encourage them to illustrate and color the stamps in any way they wish and to write a small number on each to indicate its value. Have children cut out their stamps and place them in small zippered plastic bags. They will have a lot of fun trading stamps with friends and gluing the new stamps on their stamp-collecting booklet covers and pages. Encourage children to take their booklets home and also collect canceled stamps from family members and friends.

How Many Letters in the Mailbox?

Materials

- Crayons and markers
- Paper and pencil
- Rope
- Scissors and glue
- Sealed, used envelopes with pretend mailing addresses
- Shoe boxes
- Stapler

Getting Ready: Make several mailboxes out of shoe boxes. On each box, cut one of the end panels along the sides and bottom edge to make a flap that can be raised and lowered. Make a handle out of a small piece of rope and attach it to the bottom of the flap. Mark each mailbox with a number.

Prepare a copy of the *In My Mailbox* booklet on pages 112–114 for each child. Cut out the envelopes on page 114 to be used with each booklet.

Activity: Set the mailboxes and pretend-mail envelopes on a table. Let children deliver the corresponding number of pieces of mail to each mailbox as shown on its flap.

Extend the activity by having each child complete a prepared booklet. Following the directions provided on the pattern pages, children should draw pictures and glue the correct number of envelopes on the booklet pages.

Delivering the Mail

Materials

- Glue and scissors
- Markers
- Paper
- Picture book as listed
- Self-addressed stamped envelopes

Getting Ready

- Send a letter home to parents requesting self-addressed stamped envelopes.

Introduce the lesson by talking about what happens once a stamped envelope is dropped into an official mailbox. Read aloud the book *Flat Stanley* by Jeff Brown (HarperCollins, 2006). Let children recall how Flat Stanley mailed himself across the country to visit his family. Continue the discussion by having children imagine what might happen if they mailed themselves to somewhere else. Distribute paper and let children write or dictate letters to themselves. Fold each one and insert it into each child's self-addressed stamped envelope. Point out the correct placement of the stamp on each envelope.

As a class, make a big thank-you card to give to the letter carrier who delivers the mail to your school. Also, have children learn the song "Mail Myself to You" (words and music by Woodie Guthrie, Tro-Ludlow Music, Inc., 1962) or the "Goin' on a Delivery" action rhyme provided below.

On the predetermined day, time the class's visit to the mailbox to be just before the mail carrier arrives. While presenting the thank-you card to the postal worker, sing the song or chant the rhyme. Finally, give the mail carrier the sealed envelopes that contain the children's written correspondence. Everyone will be eager to receive a special letter at home!

Goin' on a Delivery

Chant the following rhyme using a steady beat. Say each line of the rhyme and then children repeat the line as an echo.

Goin' on a delivery,
Gonna deliver the mail.
Oh, it's COLD!
I am shivering. *(Cross arms over chest and shiver.)*
Better keep movin'!

Goin' on a delivery,
Gonna deliver the mail.
Oh, it's HOT!
I'm so sweaty! *(Fan face and wipe sweat from brow.)*
Better keep movin'!

Goin' on a delivery,
Gonna deliver the mail.
Oh, it's RAINING!
I'm getting soaked! *(Pretend to put up an umbrella and then hold hand out to catch the rain.)*
Better keep movin'!

Goin' on a delivery,
Gonna deliver the mail.
Boy! It's MUDDY!
The mud is sticky! *(Lift feet up and down in place while making a "slurping" noise.)*
Better keep movin'!

Goin' on a delivery,
Gonna deliver the mail.
Yikes, It's a DOG,
a REALLY BIG DOG! *(Place palm of hand on each side of face.)*
Aiiee! Now, I'm movin'! *(Scream and wave hands overhead.)*

Materials

- Marker and chart paper
- Numbered mailboxes (see page 107)
- Stamps and ink pads
- Wrapped boxes, play money, pretend stamps, and a scale
- Writing materials

Dramatic Play Center: Our Post Office

Getting Ready: Make a chart listing weights and the related shipping costs and display it in the center. Provide copies of pretend postage stamps, play money, and a scale for children to use when "shipping" various packages.

Activity: Have children use the center for writing letters, shipping packages, mailing letters in the mailboxes, and delivering their written notes.

Community Connections

Invite a stamp collector to come and share pictures or stories about stamps and show a collection of used and/or new stamps. Additional information for inviting visitors is provided on page 6.

If possible, arrange a walking field trip to your neighborhood post office for a behind-the-scenes look at how outgoing mail is handled. While there, mail both a package and a letter to your school to see which one arrives first. Point out the postage scales to the children and buy stamps from the stamp vending machine.

Kindergarten Corner: A Message for You

Today, most mail is transported from one place to another via car, truck, or airplane. However, before these methods were available, messages were delivered or sent by other means, such as being carried by people on horses or camels or being sent by telegraph. Invite children to devise ways for sending and receiving messages in the classroom. Perhaps they might be interested in using a coded signal. Another idea would be to set up a mailbox for children to use to exchange notes with one another. Provide plenty of paper, envelopes, and stickers for stamps that children may use to write those messages. Each day, choose one child to be the letter carrier who delivers the mail.

Mail Truck *(Refer to directions on page 5 and page 166.)*

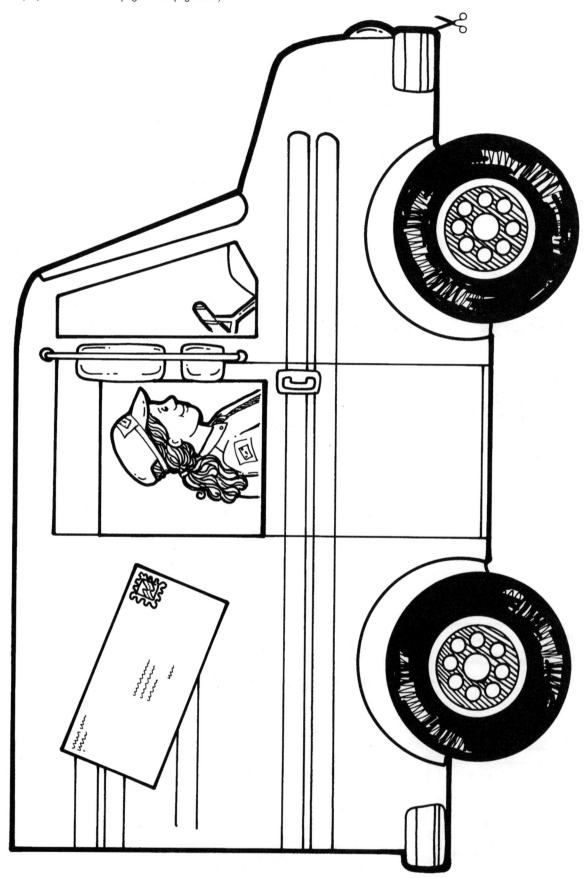

The Medical Clinic

Materials

- Construction paper
- Glue, markers, and pencils
- Picture books as listed

Getting Ready

- Make copies of the doctors on page 120. Glue each picture on a sheet of construction paper and then draw a cartoon speech bubble above it. Make one for each child.

Seeing a Doctor

Doctors and nurses help us to stay healthy. They may work in medical clinics, school health clinics, or large hospitals with lots of other people. Read aloud *My Friend the Doctor* by Joanna Cole (HarperCollins, 2005), *What to Expect When You Go to the Doctor* by Heidi Murkoff (HarperFestival, 2000), or another favorite book about doctors. Discuss the events in the story to help children recall important information about a routine checkup.

Have children think of things a doctor would tell them to do to keep their bodies healthy, such as, "eat good food," "get a lot of sleep," and "run and play outside." As each child calls out a suggestion for the doctor's advice, write the words in a speech bubble on one of the prepared pictures of doctors. Wrap up the activity by giving each child one of the papers to finish

by drawing a related picture on it. Collate and staple the completed papers together to make a class book, which may be read aloud during circle time.

Materials

- Blanket
- Marker
- Surgical masks, one for each child

Doctor, Come Quick

Have children participate in a fun group activity. Choose one child to be the doctor. Write her name on a surgical mask and help her tie it on. Direct her to stand behind a barrier so that she cannot see the rest of the group. Quietly choose another child to lie on the floor. Place a blanket over that child and remind everyone not to tell who it is. Then, together chant the following words:

> *Here lies someone who is sick, sick, sick.*
>
> *Doctor get some medicine—quick, quick, quick.*
>
> *The patient has a tummy ache—oh, oh, oh.*
>
> *Please Mr./Ms. Doctor don't be slow, slow, slow.*

Have the doctor come out from behind the barrier and try to guess who is hidden under the blanket "feeling sick." If the doctor needs a clue, the child under the blanket can say "Oh, oh, oh!" or "Help me please, doctor." When the doctor correctly guesses who is hidden under the blanket, the child who is "sick" becomes the new doctor and is given a surgical mask to wear. Continue the game until everyone has had a chance to be the doctor and the patient.

Oh, oh, oh!

Checking for Numbers

Materials

- Bathroom scale
- Crayons
- Stickers
- Tape measure

Getting Ready

- Make a copy of the booklet on pages 121 and 122 for each child.

Talk about what happens at a doctor's visit. The doctor or nurse checks for lots of different numbers when giving you an exam. First, they want to know how tall you are and how much you weigh. These numbers help the doctor know if you are healthy and growing. Other numbers the doctor checks for are your temperature, your pulse, and your age. If interested, let children weigh themselves by stepping on the scale. Give each child a copy of the *A Trip to the Doctor's Office* booklet you have prepared. Let children color the pages as desired and fill in the blanks to complete the sentences. For booklet page 2, measure the height of each child and record it. Give each child a sticker to place on page 4.

Movin' to the Beat: Glove Bop

Materials

- Music CD and player
- Surgical gloves (containing no latex)

Getting Ready

- Blow up several gloves to make "balloons" with fingers. Tie off the ends so that the air does not escape.

Play a favorite music CD while children bop the glove "balloons" into the air. Let children bop them high, bop them low, bop them fast, and bop them slow. Children can also bop them to friends or toss them in the air while lying on their backs. Let children find out if it is possible to carry a glove balloon on the palm of one hand while walking quickly. Continue dancing and bopping while time allows.

Easy Science: Sour Belly

Materials

- Antacid tablets
- Baking soda
- Plastic cups and spoons
- Water and vinegar
- Liquid soap

Getting Ready

- Fill a pitcher half full of water and then add enough vinegar to fill it. Add one squirt of liquid dish soap to the solution in the pitcher.
- Fill several bowls with baking soda.

Ask children if they have ever had a sour belly. Explain that a sour belly happens when there is too much digestive juice in the stomach. For young children, you might say that the food they eat gets mixed with tummy juices and sometimes bubbles are made. If there are too many bubbles (caused by too much acid) inside the belly, the child may get a bellyache.

Have children pair up in teams of two students. Give each team a plastic cup and a spoon. Direct children to drop a couple of spoonfuls of baking soda into their cups. Next, give each team a cup that is one-half full of the vinegar solution. CAUTION: Remind children that the antacid tablet is not candy. Then, distribute one antacid tablet to each team. Ask children to predict what will happen when they pour the liquid into the cup with the powder. Have one team member hold the cup with the vinegar solution and the other team member hold the antacid tablet. On the count of 1-2-3, have children pour the solution into the cups holding the baking powder. After watching the foam form, direct children to drop in the antacid tablets and see what happens. The medicine in the antacid "eats" away the bubbles (neutralizes the acid). Caution children that only a parent or doctor can decide when someone needs medicine.

The Children Go Marching

(Sing to the tune of "If You're Happy and You Know It")

Give each child a large bandage in its original packaging to hold while singing and following the directions below.

Put a bandage on your head, on your head. *(Tap your head twice.)*
Put a bandage on your head, on your head. *(Tap your head twice.)*
Put a bandage on your head. Put it on your head, I said.
Put a bandage on your head, on your head. *(Tap your head twice.)*

Put a bandage on your knee, on your knee. *(Tap your knee twice.)*
Put a bandage on your knee, on your knee. *(Tap your knee twice.)*
Put a bandage on your knee. It is on your knee, I see.
Put a bandage on your knee, on your knee. *(Tap your knee twice.)*

Put a bandage on your toe, on your toe. *(Tap your big toe twice.)*
Put a bandage on your toe, on your toe. *(Tap your big toe twice.)*
Put a bandage on your toe. You have 10, don't you know.
Put a bandage on your toe, on your toe. *(Tap your big toe twice.)*

Continue the song by making up other verses.

Materials

- Apples (two or three different varieties)
- Paper
- Paper plates
- Scissors and tape
- Table knife
- Toothpicks

An Apple a Day

Getting Ready: (NOTE: Follow your school's guidelines for serving foods in the classroom.) Place one whole apple in the middle of a plate, one variety per plate. Cut other apples of the same variety into small wedges and place them around the whole apple. Divide a paper plate in half with a solid line. On one side of the plate, draw a simple face shape that has a big smile. On the other side, draw a sad-looking face. Make one plate for each child. Cut several small strips of paper. Tape each one to a toothpick.

Activity: An old saying goes, "An apple a day keeps the doctor away." Ask children what they think the saying means. Explain that if you eat healthful foods, such as an apple every day, you are helping to keep your body strong.

Give each child a plate and a toothpick. Have children use their senses to explore the different kinds of apples. Talk about the apples' colors and shapes. Invite children to taste a variety of apples. After tasting each one, have them categorize the apple by placing it on the smiley-faced side of their plates if they liked it or the sad-faced side if they didn't. Ask them to describe the different apples as they taste them. Record the words on the toothpick paper strips and stick each toothpick into the corresponding apple in the center of the plate. When everyone is finished tasting, read the words on each apple to see if the class agrees with the descriptions.

Dramatic Play Center: Our Medical Clinic

Materials

- Clipboard and paper
- Cotton balls
- Magazines
- Notepad and pencils
- Small bed for an examination table
- Strips of fabric torn into bandages
- Stuffed toy animals
- Surgical masks, gloves, lab coat, and scrubs
- Tape measure and bathroom scale
- Toy doctor's kit (stethoscope, thermometer, etc.)

Consider converting a small cozy area into a "medical clinic." To set up the waiting room, arrange a few chairs and provide magazines and books for patients to read. If possible, designate another area with a small bed as the examination room and provide a toy doctor's kit along with a clipboard, notepad for "writing" prescriptions, bandages, slings, and so on. Gather a few stuffed animals to be the patients, and then all that is needed are a few good workers!

Community Connections

Invite one or more of the following people to visit your classroom: doctor, nurse, pharmacist, or paramedic. Additional information about inviting visitors is provided on page 6. If possible, plan a walking field trip to a medical clinic for a behind-the-scenes tour of the place where doctors and nurses work.

Kindergarten Corner: All in a Day's Work

Materials

- Crayons and pencils
- Picture books as listed

Getting Ready

- Make a copy of page 123 for each child.

The work of a doctor is very fascinating because the human body is quite complex, being made up of different systems: skeletal, muscular, circulatory, digestive, and so on. Talk about a few different kinds of doctors with the class. Point out that some doctors work with children only. They are called pediatricians. Some doctors are surgeons and work in hospitals, specializing in fixing certain parts of the body: weak hearts, broken bones, crooked noses, and so on. Read aloud *Big Book of the Human Body* (DK Publishing, 2006) or *Me and My Amazing Body* by Joan Sweeney (Dragonfly Books, 2000).

Distribute a copy of the "Keeping What's Inside Healthy" poster to each child. Help children recall what they learned about the human body from the picture book. Then, on the backs of the papers, have children "write" stories about ways they can keep their bodies healthy, such as running and playing to make their hearts and bones strong.

Ambulance *(Refer to directions on page 5 and page 166.)*

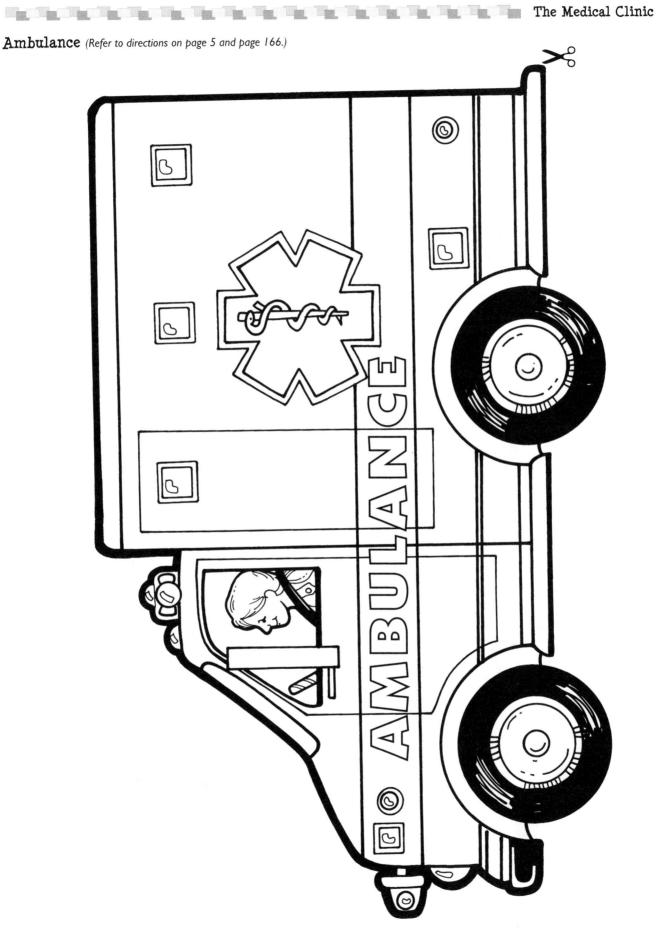

Seeing a Doctor Patterns *(Refer to directions on page 115.)*

120

To the teacher: Make one copy of the booklet (pages 121 and 122) for each child. Cut out each page along the dashed lines. Collate the booklet pages and staple them together. On page 2, measure and have the child finish the sentence.

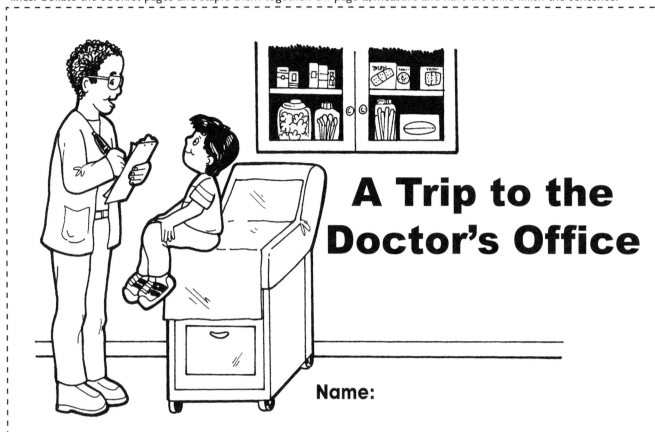

A Trip to the Doctor's Office

Name:

My doctor wants to know if I am growing. The nurse checks to see how tall I am. She finds out how much I weigh.

I am _____ tall.   **2**

To the teacher: On page 3, have the child finish the sentence. On page 4, give the child a sticker to place under the words "Way to Go!"

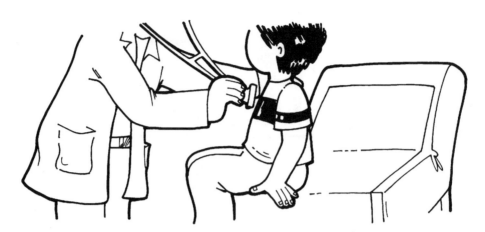

My doctor listens to the beats of my heart and then says, "My, you're getting big. How old are you?"

I am _____ years old.

3

If I'm brave, I get a sticker!
I like to visit the doctor.

4

All in a Day's Work Poster *(Refer to directions on page 118.)*

Keeping What's Inside Healthy

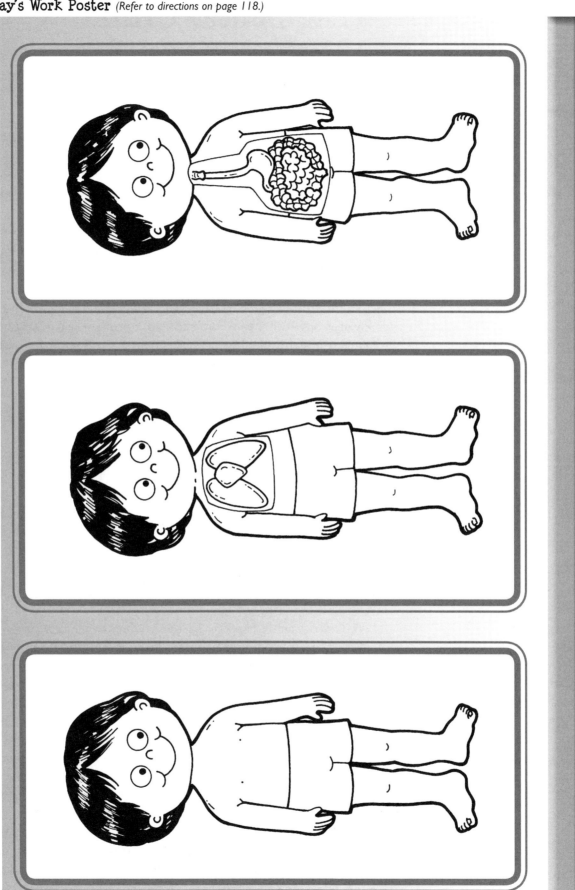

The Dental Clinic

Materials

- Costume teeth and toothbrush
- Picture books as listed
- Stuffed toy animals

Getting Ready

- Visit the American Dental Association and the Canadian Dental Association Web sites to learn more how the bacteria in plaque can cause tooth decay and about good oral hygiene techniques.

Dentists at Work

A dentist is someone who helps people take care of their teeth. Tell children that dentists will also fix teeth when needed. Read *Doctor De Soto* by William Steig (Farrar, Straus and Giroux, 1990), *Going to the Dentist* by Dawn Sirett (DK Publishing, 2007) or a favorite book about a dentist at work. Encourage discussion about the importance of taking good care of our teeth. Point out that we use them to chew food and to keep our lips in the right place when we talk.

When we eat food, particularly those foods with a lot of sugar in them, food particles stick to our teeth. This forms plaque, which can make tiny little holes (cavities) in a tooth's hard outer layer (called the enamel). The best thing to do to avoid getting cavities in your teeth is to eat healthful foods, drink water between meals, and brush your teeth at least two times each day. Demonstrate with stuffed toy animals how to brush teeth. If possible, also use a model of human teeth to demonstrate the technique. Let children take turns being the dentist and explaining the proper ways to take care of teeth.

Materials

- 2 fresh eggs
- 2 clear containers
- Baby teeth
- Carbonated cola drink (not diet) in a glass
- Vinegar

Easy Science: Sugary Snacks and Teeth

Let's find out what happens to teeth when too much sugar stays in the mouth. Set up an experiment to demonstrate how the enamel coating gets eaten away by the acids produced by bacteria in plaque. Show everyone a fresh egg and let them carefully feel the eggshell. Talk about how the shell is hard, just like their teeth. Then, place the egg in a container filled with vinegar. Set the second egg in a separate empty container. Check the eggs the next day. Have children feel the difference in the shell of the egg that has been sitting in the vinegar bath overnight and the second egg. Discuss the results. Return the first egg to the vinegar and check the eggs daily for three to five days. Explain that the shell of an egg is made out of calcium, which is similar to enamel. Because our teeth are much harder, the decaying process takes a longer time, but the effect is similar. Discard everything when finished with the experiment.

Alternatively, show the damaging effects of sugar on teeth by placing baby teeth in a glass of soda. After a few weeks, there will be a noticeable effect on the teeth. Discard all liquids and teeth when finished with the experiment.

Healthy Teeth Count

Materials

- Digital camera
- Golf tees
- Molding dough
- Picture book as listed
- Plastic mirror
- Polystyrene packaging in pieces

When you visit a dental clinic, the dentist will check your teeth to see that they are healthy. The dentist will also count your teeth and sometimes will use a special camera to take a picture (called an X-ray) of your teeth. Begin the activity by taking a close-up picture of each child showing a big toothy grin. Then, let children use a mirror to count their teeth. As everyone totals the amount, they may be amazed to know that most children have 20 baby teeth while most adults have 32. Develop the pictures in a 5" x 7" (13 cm x 18 cm) or larger format and then display them in your dramatic play center. Read aloud the book *The Berenstain Bears Visit the Dentist* by Stan and Jan Berenstain (Random House, 1981) and encourage a dialogue about Dr. Bearson filling Brother Bear's cavity.

Unlike sharks, adult human teeth if lost do not grow back. That is why it is important to take good care of our big teeth to keep them strong. Explain to children that if they do have a cavity, it can be filled by a dentist to stop its damage to the tooth. Give each child a piece of polystyrene. Have children poke holes in their pieces with golf tees. Then, let them practice being "dentists" by filling the holes with molding dough. Continue filling holes until the "teeth" are completely fixed.

Materials

- Crayons and pencil
- New toothbrush
- Dental floss and tape
- Picture book as listed
- Scissors
- String and small beads or stapler

Getting Ready

- Make a copy of *My Tooth Book* on pages 128–131 for each child. Before cutting out the pages, decide if they will be tooth shaped or rectangular. If making a rectangular booklet, simply collate and staple the pages together.

Making a "Toothy" Book

Begin the lesson by reading aloud the book *How Many Teeth?* by Paul Showers (HarperTrophy, 1991). Perhaps some of the children have already lost teeth and are fascinated about what will happen to those gaps between their baby teeth. Use the chart in the book to show how big teeth develop under the baby teeth.

Conclude the lesson by making toothy booklets with children. (Complete the booklet pages as directed on the pattern pages.) Cut out, collate, and then punch a hole through the tops of the tooth-shaped pages. Thread a length of string through the holes and secure it by knotting the ends together. (Optional: Insert a small bead on the string between each page to make it easier to turn the pages.)

Toothy Snack

Materials

- Peanut butter or caramel dipping sauce
- Miniature marshmallows
- Plastic knives
- Red apples
- Small plates

Getting Ready: (NOTE: Follow your school's guidelines for serving food in the classroom.) Check for food allergies and make alternative arrangements to substitute caramel dipping sauce for the peanut butter if necessary.

Activity: Cut the apples into wedges and then give each child two wedges along with a handful of miniature marshmallows. Have children spread peanut butter on the apple wedges with a knife. Invite them to count each marshmallow as they stick the marshmallow "teeth" into the peanut butter. Stack one apple wedge on top of the other so that the teeth meet in the middle and then enjoy the "toothy smile" as a snack.

Some Fun with the Tooth Fairy

Materials

- Card stock
- Pillows
- Scissors and markers

Getting Ready

- Cut a tooth shape out of card stock.
- For the lost tooth game, cut out 20 teeth from card stock. Label 10 teeth with a numeral from 1–10. On the remaining teeth, draw or use stickers to show the corresponding sets.

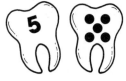

Talk about the fact that when children are about six years old, they start to lose their baby teeth and new permanent teeth grow in. One legendary figure is the Tooth Fairy who, it is said, will sneak into a child's room at night and exchange money for a lost tooth if the tooth is put it under the child's pillow. Children all over the world have different traditions that they celebrate when they lose a tooth. Read aloud *Throw Your Tooth on the Roof: Tooth Traditions from Around the World* by Selby Beeler (Houghton Mifflin, 2001) to discover the interesting things that children living in other countries do with their baby teeth when they lose them.

Whether children believe the Tooth Fairy is real or not, it is fun to imagine waking up to a surprise! Place several pillows on the floor around the room. Have children cover their eyes while you hide the tooth shape you have prepared. Let them race to find under which pillow the tooth is hiding.

Extend the fun with "lost teeth" by playing a game. Hide 20 teeth labeled with sets and numerals all around the classroom. Direct each child to find one or two teeth and then locate the classmates who have the corresponding teeth, matching each numeral to the correct set of dots.

Dramatic Play Center: Our Dental Clinic

Materials

- Chairs
- Dental tools (no picks)
- Magazines and books
- Models of teeth
- New toothbrushes
- Paper napkins and metal paper clips
- Plastic hand mirror
- Stickers
- Stuffed toy animals
- Surgical face masks, one for each child, and rubber gloves
- Swivel arm lamp
- TV tray table

Children can have lots of fun playing the role of a dentist or hygienist and caring for patients. Arrange a few chairs and magazines to make a "waiting room." Then, on the other side of the play space, set up one chair, a TV tray table and a swivel arm lamp (if allowed in your classroom). Have children take turns donning their own face masks and rubber gloves. Your young dentists will be eager to examine the stuffed-animal patients and brush their teeth. CAUTION: Be sure to remind children that the instruments and toothbrushes should only be used on the stuffed animals—not people—so that no germs are spread.

Community Connections

Invite one or more of the following people to your classroom: dentist, dental hygienist, or lab technician. Additional information for inviting visitors is provided on page 6.

If possible, arrange an excursion for the class to a neighborhood dental office for a behind-the-scenes tour of the place where dentists and dental hygienists work.

Kindergarten Corner: Kinds of Teeth

Materials

- Model or pictures of teeth
- Picture book as listed
- Plastic mirror
- White molding dough

Adults have more teeth than children. Tell students that no matter the number of teeth you have, each one has a specific job. The teeth in the front of your mouth are shaped like chisels and are used for biting. The canines—sharp teeth that separate your front teeth and your molars—are for ripping and tearing. Your back teeth are called molars. They are used to crush and mash food into little pieces so that your stomach can digest it. Read aloud *Look! My Tooth Is Loose!* by Patricia Brennan Demuth (Grosset & Dunlap, 2002) to clarify what each kind of tooth does.

Using white molding dough, children can make models of teeth. The crown of each front tooth should have a single, sharp edge, and molars should have tiny bumps. It is very helpful for children to be able to examine their teeth with a mirror while they are working. Perhaps, they might form enough teeth for a whole mouthful!

To the teacher: Make one copy of the booklet (pages 128–131) for each child. Cut out each page along the dashed lines or around the shape of the tooth. *(To assemble the booklet, refer to page 125.)*

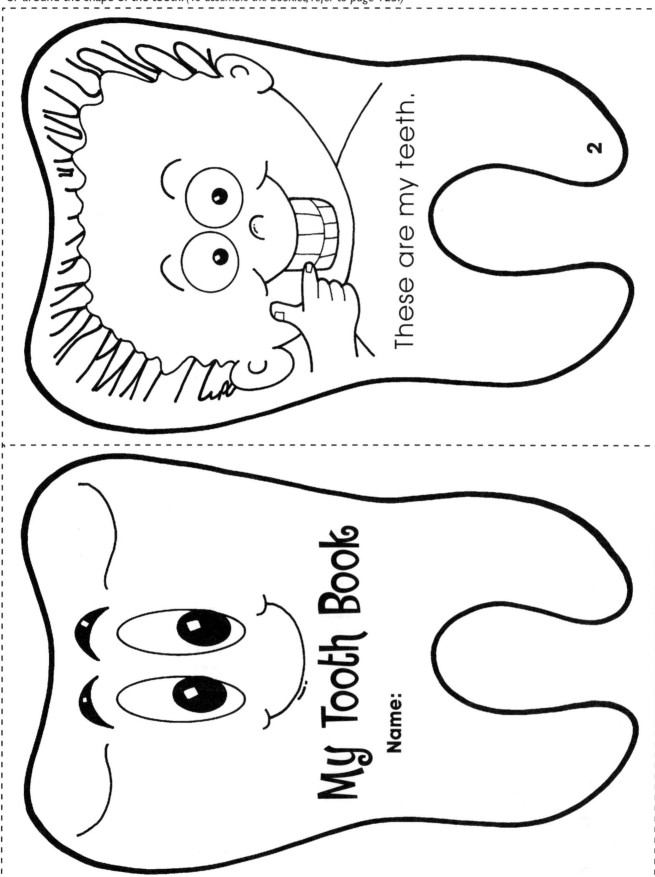

These are my teeth.

2

My Tooth Book

Name:

To the teacher: On page 3, have the child brush the tooth with a new toothbrush. On page 4, have the child tape a piece of floss onto the tooth.

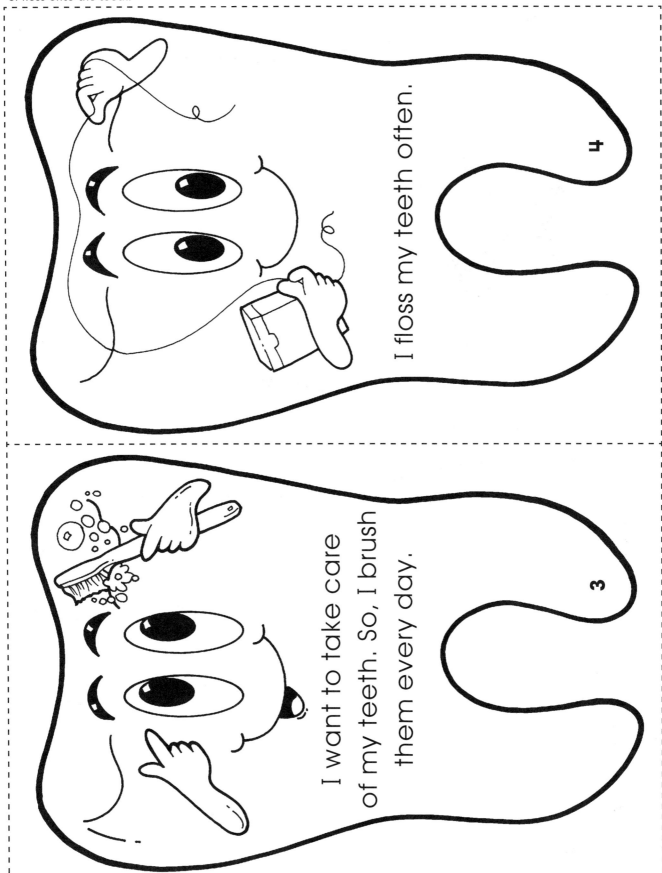

I floss my teeth often.

4

I want to take care of my teeth. So, I brush them every day.

3

To the teacher: On page 5, have the child clip pictures of healthful foods from grocery store fliers and glue them onto the tooth. On page 6, have the child draw a smiley face on the page after "reading" the sentence.

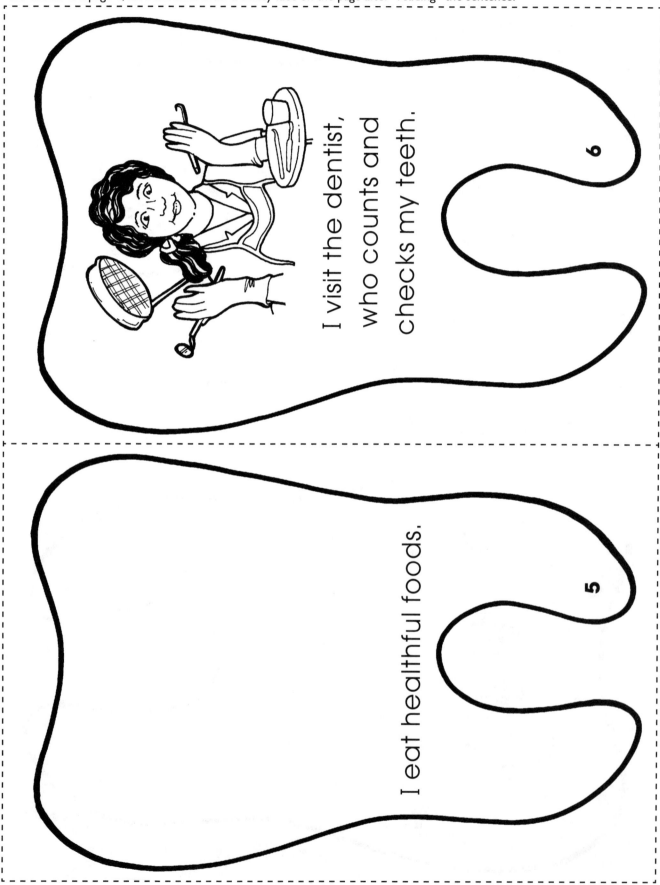

I visit the dentist, who counts and checks my teeth.

6

I eat healthful foods.

5

To the teacher: On page 7, have the child use a mirror to count the teeth. Then, fill in the blanks and circle the correct word accordingly. On page 8, have the child draw a self-portrait.

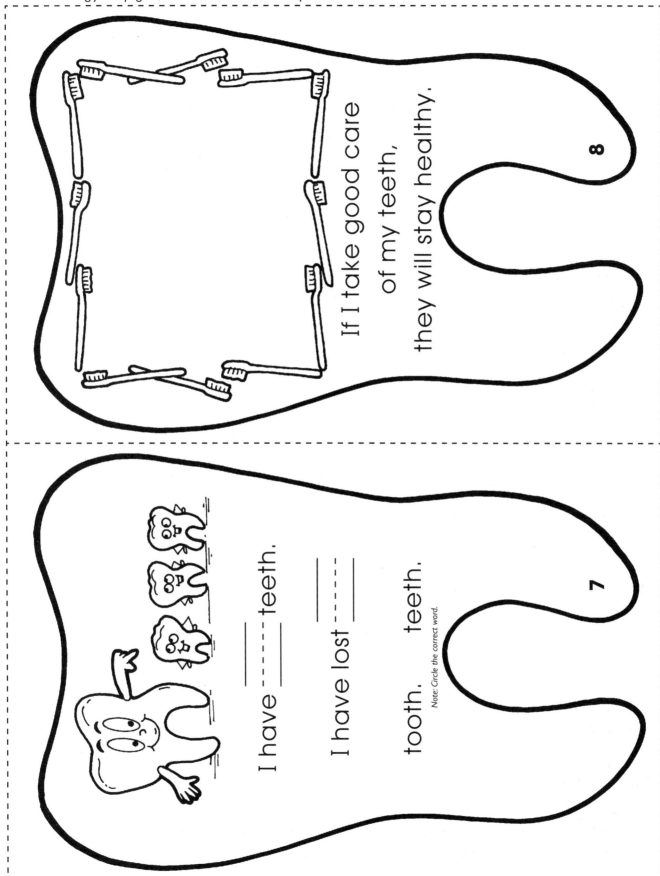

If I take good care of my teeth, they will stay healthy.

8

I have _____ teeth.

I have lost _____

tooth.　teeth.

Note: Circle the correct word.

7

The Animal Health Clinic

Materials

- Crayons or markers
- Picture books as listed
- Stuffed toy animals

Taking My Pet to See the Vet

Getting Ready: Make a copy of the booklet on pages 136 and 137 for each child. Cut out the pages along the dashed lines. Collate and staple the booklet pages along the left edge of the paper.

Activity: Just like people, pets need to see doctors, too. Talk about that sometimes pets get sick or they need checkups to find out if they are growing well and staying healthy. A veterinarian is a doctor for animals. Read aloud *My Cat Is Going to the Dogs* by Mike Thaler (Troll Communications, 1999) or *Bark, George* by Jules Feiffer (HarperCollins Publishers, 1999) for some surprising outcomes of visits to the veterinarian.

Veterinarians do not just work with pets. Some vets work with zoo animals, while others take care of farm animals. These doctors go to the animals' homes for checkups. (It is very difficult to bring an elephant to see a vet!) Show the class various stuffed toy animals. Discuss with children which animals might be seen by a vet. Wrap up the discussion by giving each child a copy of the booklet *A Pet Goes to the Vet* and talk about the pictures. Have children draw a picture on page 2 and then color the scenes as desired.

Materials

- Colorful card stock
- Scissors
- Zippered plastic bag

Getting Ready

- Using colorful card stock, make four copies of the animal picture cards on page 138 for each group of four players. Cut out the cards along the dashed lines and store them in a zippered plastic bag.

Card Game: Go to the Vet

This card game is similar to Go Fish with a fun twist. To begin the game with a group of four children, deal six cards to each player. Stack the remaining cards facedown in the center of the playing area to make a draw pile. All players should look at their cards and lay down any sets of two or four cards with the same picture. Players take turns requesting cards from other players to complete additional sets. However, rather than saying the animal's name, a player makes the animal's sound or action when requesting a card. For example, Player A might request a cat card from Player C by saying, "Do you have a MEOW?" If Player C does not have the requested card, she says, "Go to the vet," and then Player A will pick up a card from the draw pile to finish the turn. If Player C does have the card, it is given to Player A. The game continues until all cards have been matched into sets of two or four cards. The winner is the player who collects the most sets of cards.

Materials

- Beads
- Cardboard boxes, one per child
- Chenille stems
- Construction paper
- Craft foam sheets
- Crayons
- Markers
- Scissors
- Stuffed toy animals, one per child

Getting Ready

- Cut rectangles of craft foam, 1.5" x 4" (4 cm x 10 cm), one for each child.
- Punch a hole near one of the edges of each foam rectangle.

Adopt a Pet

Sometimes, pets get lost and are not found by their owners. Or, sometimes things happen so that owners can no longer take good care of their pets. A pet shelter is a place where homeless pets can stay until a new owner is found. Just like at the animal health clinic, a veterinarian may examine these homeless pets. The vet makes sure the animals are healthy and that they have had their shots in preparation for being adopted into new homes. Perhaps the children can share stories about adopting pets from animal shelters.

Have each child choose a "rescued pet" from the stuffed animals you have collected. The child, acting as a veterinarian, may check the pet by looking at its eyes, nose, mouth, and ears; by feeling its tummy; and by checking its feet and tail. Children can also pretend to wash the pets in a dishpan, scrubbing the animals with rags and "drying" them with towels.

Give each child a craft foam rectangle, one or more chenille stems, and a handful of beads. Let the child think of a name for the rescued pet and write it on the foam rectangle with a marker. Have children make pet collars, stringing beads on the chenille stems and then adding the name tags. Use as many stems as necessary for the size of the pet. Have the child twist the collar around the rescued pet and then place it into a cardboard box to keep the pet safe.

When the animals are ready for "adoption," invite children to draw pictures of their rescued pets on sheets of construction paper. Ask them to dictate or write descriptions about their animals and add them to their pictures to create "found" posters. After the children share their posters with the rest of the class, tape them on the wall above the animals in their boxes.

You may want to extend the activity by switching the stuffed animals around into different boxes. Tell the class that there has been a problem at the animal shelter. Explain that some animals were placed in the wrong cages after the cages were cleaned by the workers! Let children fix the problem.

At the end of the week, have the rescued pets get "adopted" and let children keep the pet collars they made.

Community Connections

Invite a veterinarian and/or animal health assistant to visit your classroom. Additional information for inviting guests is provided on page 6.

If possible, arrange for the class to take a walking field trip to an animal health clinic for a behind-the-scenes tour.

My Pet Loves the Vet

(Sing to the tune of "My Bonnie Lies over the Ocean")

My doggy [or another kind of pet] was feeling quite yucky. *(Frown and rub your tummy.)*
I took my pet to the vet. *(Pretend to cradle a pet in your arms.)*
The vet checked my pet—head to toes. *(Touch head and toes.)*
And now my pet's fine, don't you know. *(Hold hands out with palms up while shrugging shoulders.)*

Dogs, cats, gerbils, rats,
A vet helps your pet stay healthy, too.
Birds, snakes, bunnies, pigs,
My pet loves his vet, don't you?

Materials

- Assortment of snack crackers
- Index cards and marker
- Plastic food server gloves
- Small bowls

Getting Ready

- Place an assortment of snack crackers (fish-shaped crackers, cheese squares, pretzels, etc.) into small bowls with each kind of snack in a separate bowl.
- Write a numeral on an index card and tape it to the front of a bowl. Each bowl should have a different numeral.

Kitty Kibble, Puppy Chow

Pets need food to eat, but they also enjoy treats. Treats are often offered to pets for good behavior or for performing tricks. Have children make their own pet treats. (NOTE: Follow your school's guidelines for serving foods in the classroom.) Have children wash their hands. Then, give each child an empty bowl and a pair of food server gloves. On a table, set out an assortment of snacks in bowls that have been labeled with numerals. Direct children to fill their pet treat dishes with different snacks by looking at the numeral on each food bowl and then counting out that corresponding number of snacks. For example, if the pretzel bowl is labeled with the numeral 5, the child would count out five pretzels to add to the pet treat dish. Continue counting and mixing snack items until everyone has a dish full of tasty "pet treats."

Pair up children for this activity. Have one child be the "pet owner" and the other child the "pet." Have the owner give the pet a command such as "sit," "roll over," "jump 10 times," etc. After the pet performs the command, the pet is given a treat from his dish. Switch roles so that the pet can become the owner. Continue the activity until all treats are gone.

Flea Stomp

Every once in a while a pet will pick up tiny insect pests called "fleas." Fleas are little insects that bite the skin of the animal they live on. You may notice your pet scratching a lot, and if you do not get rid of them, fleas can get on you!

Play this fun movement activity to get rid of fleas! Take the small paper circles you have prepared and spread them across a large play area. These are the "fleas." Play a lively music selection, such as "Spanish Flea" from *The Very Best of Herb Alpert* (Universal Int'l, 1999). Have children pretend to scratch an imaginary itch that moves all over their bodies. Call out names of body parts to scratch as they dance to the music. Periodically, turn off or pause the music and call out a number. Then, have children stomp on that corresponding number of "fleas" on the floor. Continue scratching and stomping until the music ends. When everyone is all "stomped out," have children pick up all the "fleas" and count them together to find out how many were collected.

Dramatic Play Center: Our Animal Health Clinic

When setting up your "animal health clinic," locate a set of toy doctor tools and other related materials for young "veterinarians" to use. Nearby, designate a spot as an animal shelter for any stray animals that need a good home. An area for grooming pets can easily be set up by providing brushes, towels, a dishpan for pet "baths," and so on. Supply small boxes made to look like crates and clean bowls for "feeding" pets being kenneled in the clinic for fun, imaginative play.

Kindergarten Corner: Lost and Found

Write the word *Lost* at the top of a piece of paper and the word *Reward* on the bottom. Make a copy of the paper for each child.

Announce to the class that some pets are missing! Let each child select a photo of a favorite stuffed animal and paste it in the middle of the paper. To help others identify the "missing pets," each child should dictate or write a description of the selected animal beneath the photo. Finish the poster by writing a dollar amount for the reward at the bottom of the paper. Give each child some play money. Then, have pairs of children swap posters and invite them to search around the room for their partners' animals. Whenever a pet is found, its owner then pays the child the reward for finding it.

To the teacher: Make a copy of the booklet (on pages 136 and 137) for each child. Cut out each page along the dashed lines. Collate the booklet pages and staple them together. On page 2, have the child draw a picture of a pet in the scene.

My Pet Goes to the Vet

A vet helps pets.
Draw your pet in the picture.

2

This pet is sick. The vet will help him feel better soon. Thank you, Vet!

3

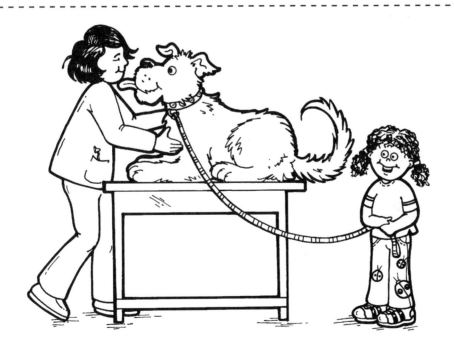

This pet is healthy. The vet gives her shots so she won't get sick. Thank you, Vet!

4

Go to the Vet Game Cards *(Refer to directions on page 132.)*

Landfill & Recycling Center

Materials

- Empty bins
- Items that can be recycled
- Glue
- Paints and markers
- Picture book as listed
- Scissors and tape

Getting Ready

- A week or so before doing this activity, send home a note requesting parents to donate clean, empty recyclable packaging to the school.

Use It Again

Once children are seated on the floor in a circle, dump the collected recyclable products into the middle of the area. Read aloud the book *Smash! Mash! Crash! There Goes the Trash!* by Barbara Odanaka (Margaret K. McElderry Books, 2006) or another book about trash collecting. Discuss the process that trash undergoes as it is moved from the home to its final destination. To reduce the huge volume of things that are thrown away each day, some of those items could be reused or recycled.

Talk about the items that are on the floor in the middle of the circle of children. You might discuss how they were used and what new products can be made from those materials. Newspaper and other paper products can be made into new paper. Plastic containers and bottles can be melted down and spun into fibers to make clothes, park benches, blankets, and so on. Aluminum soda cans can be melted down and made into new soda cans.

Have children take turns sorting the items into piles so that all plastic items are in one pile, all metal items are in a second pile, and all paper products are in a third pile. Place a few items from each pile on a table along with glue, tape, paint, and markers. Encourage children to create artworks of abstract sculpture using a few of the recycled products. Let them explore and discover which items can be taped together easily, which can be cut, which can be painted, and so on. When each work of art is completed, have the child tell you about the finished project and then place it on a table or shelf for display.

Materials

- 2 trash cans
- Garbage bags
- Poster board and marker
- Scale

Getting Ready

- Create a grid chart with two columns. Above one column write "Trash." Above the other column write "Recycle."
- Label one trash can "recycle" and the other "trash."

Weigh the Trash

To assess how much trash is discarded and how much is recycled in your classroom, create a class chart to record the output of trash over the course of a week. Place two trash cans in the room—one for regular trash and one for recyclables. Each day, remove the garbage bag with the trash in it and place it on the scale. If the bag is too large, have a child hold the bag while standing on a bathroom scale. Then, have the child stand alone on the scale and subtract the difference in weight. Record the weight of the trash on the chart. Repeat the process for all recycled products. At the end of the week, total the number of pounds of trash and of recyclables and compare the two amounts. Brainstorm with children to think of other ways they can recycle even more of the discarded classroom items.

T-Shirt Pillows

Getting Ready: A week before this unit, send home a parent letter requesting a child's used T-shirt for each child. Label each T-shirt's tag or inside the neckline with the child's name and wash the shirts, along with any pillows that were donated, in hot water with soap and a chlorine bleach additive.

Solicit parent help to prepare the T-shirts for the project. To turn the T-shirt into a pillowcase, first turn the shirt inside out. Close the neckline, the bottom of the shirt, and one of the sleeves by stitching along those edges with a sewing machine. Turn the shirt right side out and slip a section of newspaper into the shirt to prevent fabric paint from bleeding through as the child decorates it.

Activity: Another way to recycle is to reuse something old in a new way. Read aloud the book *Something from Nothing* by Phoebe Gilman (Scholastic Canada, 2008) about a grandfather who recycles a child's blanket into many other useful things. Share any examples you have of objects that have been usefully recycled, such as a tin can pencil holder or a tote bag made from a pair of jeans.

Return each prepared T-shirt pillowcase to its owner. Begin by talking about wearing the T-shirts—whether they were favorite shirts or if the shirts remind children of special experiences. After discussing the shirts, let children decorate them as desired with fabric paints. Once the paint has dried thoroughly, remove the newspaper and stuff the pillows with cotton batting until each one is fluffy and full. Finally, to finish each pillow close the opening of the sleeve by hand sewing a seam along its edge. Let children show their recycled pillows during circle time.

Materials

- Cotton batting or pillows
- Fabric paint
- Needle and thread
- Newspapers
- Paintbrushes
- Picture book as listed
- Sewing machine
- Used T-shirts

Will It Decay?

What happens to the trash that is picked up by a garbage truck? Brainstorm ideas with children and then explain that in some places, each load of trash may be hauled to a spot called a "landfill" where it is buried under huge piles of dirt and sand. Read aloud *I Drive a Garbage Truck* by Sarah Bridges (Picture Window Books, 2005) or another book about the day in the life of a garbage truck.

Eventually, some of the things in a landfill will turn into dirt (the good stuff). Introduce the word *biodegradable* to the children, explaining that some things slowly change, or *decay*, into very small particles that can be found in soil. To find out which things will decay, gather an assortment of trash materials. Place each item in a small plastic container and invite children to predict which things they think will decay. (Here is a hint: If something is organic, it will biodegrade.) Write the name of each item on a craft stick. Then, write the word *yes* on the stick if children think it will decay or the word *no* if they think it will not decay. Remove each item from its container and then fill it half full with soil. To make each item visible, place it in the soil inside the container along the outer edge. Add a small amount of water to the soil when dry. Be patient; it will take several weeks for some items to biodegrade. Discard all containers when finished.

Materials

- Dirt (not potting soil)
- Jumbo-size craft sticks and marker
- Picture book as listed
- Small, clear plastic containers
- Various trash materials, such as newspaper, plastic bags, apple peelings, banana slices or peels, etc.

Garbage Can Romp

Materials

• Child's wagon
• One very large plastic garbage can with lid (new or very clean)

Place the garbage can in the middle of the room. Have children sit in a circle around the outside of the garbage can. Choose one child to come forward. Give the child a direction such as, "Go around the garbage can." Other directions may include "Stand beside the garbage can" or "Get inside the garbage can." Continue playing until everyone has had a chance to participate.

Alternatively, have children collect "trash" from around the room based on criteria you give them. Set the garbage can in the wagon and let the child pull the wagon to the object for collecting. (Consider having two or three children work together to manage the garbage can.)

Community Connections

Make arrangements for the class to watch what happens when the garbage truck picks up the trash at your school. If possible, take the class on a field trip to a recycling center. Before touring the facility, read aloud the book *Where Does the Garbage Go?* by Paul Showers (HarperCollins Publishers, 1994).

Dramatic Play Center: Taking Care of the Trash

Materials

• Child-sized shovel
• Clean, empty, recyclable containers
• Craft paper and markers
• Garbage bags
• Newspaper
• Small trash cans
• Wagon
• Work gloves

Your young "sanitation workers" will have lots of fun in the dramatic play center loading and unloading the trash. Use markers on large sheets of craft paper to create different house fronts. Tape the "buildings" up around the play area. Place a small trash can next to each house. Fill the trash cans with wadded-up newspaper or clean recyclable containers. Let children use a small wagon as a "garbage truck" and pull it around the center, stopping at the houses and dumping the trash into it. (Remind them to make a beeping noise when they back up!) Take the trash to another area in the play space and sort the recyclable items into predetermined groups.

Kindergarten Corner: Swap Meet

Getting Ready: Send home a note requesting families to donate one toy item to school that the child no longer wants or needs. Explain that each child will bring a toy and "swap" it for another friend's toy.

Activity: Talk with children about a different way to recycle items, rather than throwing them in the trash. Point out that it is possible to give things to someone else who can use them. On the designated day, place the donated items on a table and have children take turns choosing a toy to take home. Any additional toys can be donated to a charity organization of your choice.

File Folder Game: Garbage Pickup

Materials

- 4 small paper cups
- Card stock
- Clear packing tape
- Colorful copier paper
- Die
- File folder
- Markers
- Scissors and glue
- Small bowl
- Small pieces of colored paper
- Small plastic box with lid

Getting Ready

1. Make one copy of this page and the game board on pages 144 and 145 on colorful copier paper. Using card stock, make four copies of the garbage truck game marker on this page. Color the trucks, each one a different color, and cut them out. Cut out the "To Play" instruction box.

2. Open the folder and orient it so that the tab is on the right. Write the name of the game on the tab. Trim around the game board scene pieces as desired. Glue the two scene pieces to the file folder so that the borders meet at the center of the fold, making one continuous path through the town. Write a numeral 1–5 on the door of each house.

3. Close the folder and glue the "To Play" instruction box on the front panel.

4. Optional: Laminate the entire file folder and the garbage truck game markers for durability. Trim around the edges.

5. Tape each small garbage truck to the front of a paper cup. Crumple small pieces of colored paper to form small balls.

6. Store the truck game marker cups, die, and paper balls in a small plastic box along with the game board.

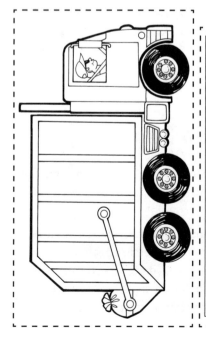

To Play

1. Place your truck on "Start." Put the garbage balls in a small bowl.

2. Take turns rolling the die and moving the same number of spaces as shown.

3. If you stop in front of a house, pick up the same number of garbage balls as shown on the door.

4. When all trucks stop at the recycling center, dump out the garbage and count the balls.

Garbage Truck *(Refer to directions on page 5 and page 166.)*

Don's Trash Service

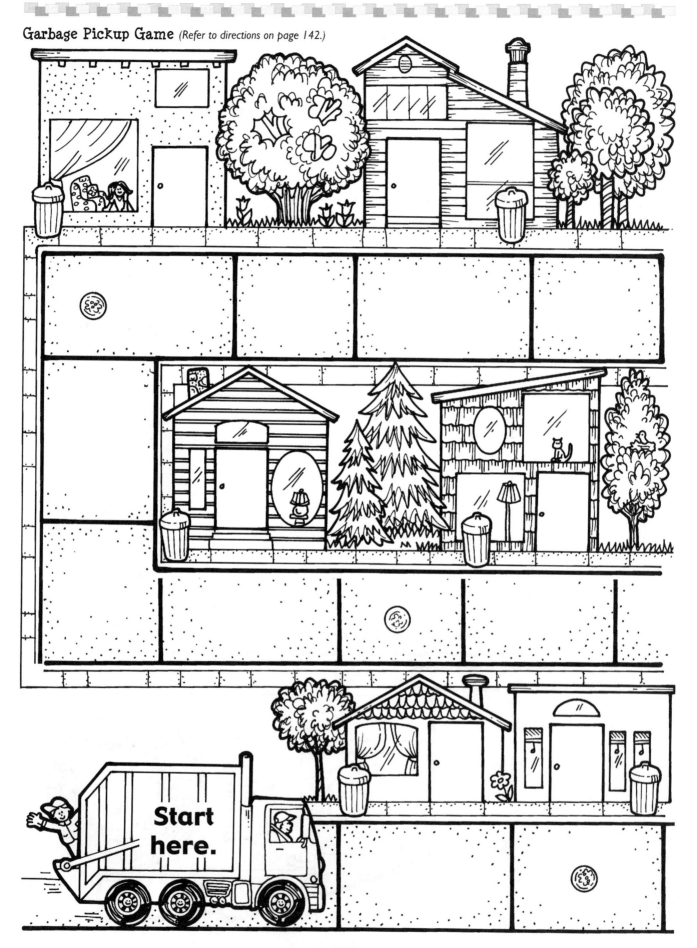

Start here.

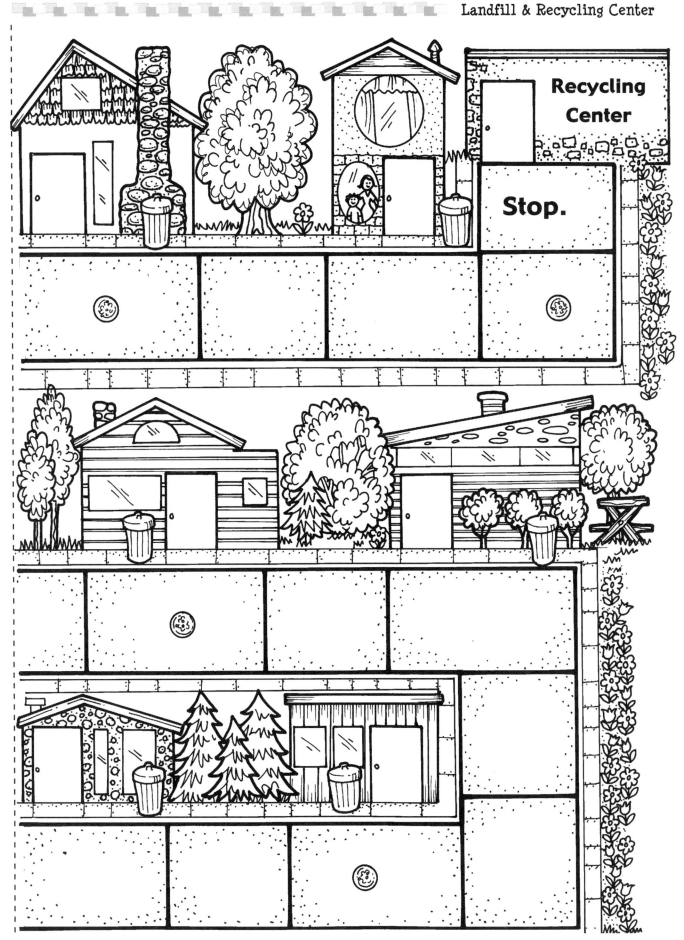

Recycling Center

Stop.

145 *All Around the Neighborhood*

Construction Sites

Construction Zone

Materials

- Large foil baking pans or sand table
- Dirt and gravel
- Sticks and blocks
- Paper and crayons
- Picture books as listed

Read aloud *The Lot at the End of My Block* by Kevin Lewis (Hyperion, 2001); *One Big Building: A Counting Book About Construction* by Michael Dahl (Picture Window Books, 2004); *Mike Mulligan and His Steam Shovel* by Virginia Lee Burton (Houghton Mifflin, 2007); *Construction Zone* by Tana Hoban (Greenwillow, 1997); or another book about building structures and other kinds of construction projects. Talk about the kinds of jobs that construction workers do. Some workers build roads or bridges, some workers build homes or other buildings. It takes many different kinds of skills to complete one construction job. For example, in order to build a home, talk about the workers who excavate the site, pour the concrete foundation, build the frame, install electrical wiring or plumbing fixtures, shingle the roof, and so on—just to name a few steps of the project. Then, have children imagine what kind of project they would build if they were a construction worker. Have them draw a picture of their construction project and write or dictate a story about it. What kind of structure is it? How will it be used?

In small groups, have children work together to create their own buildings. Begin by providing foil baking pans containing dirt. First, children must dig and smooth the dirt. Then, they may "create" a building with blocks or other building materials. Gravel can be used for sidewalks and roads to the new construction site.

Tool Tracks

Materials

- Bottles of red, blue, and yellow food coloring
- Ingredients for molding dough
- Rolling pin
- Tools (small hammer, screwdriver, extra large screws, etc.)
- Toy construction trucks

Getting Ready: Make a batch of molding dough and color it brown. (Use your favorite recipe or locate one on the Internet.) The color brown can be made by mixing together drops of red, blue, and yellow food coloring.

Activity: Give each child a large ball of molding dough. Place a construction truck and the assortment of tools on the table. First, flatten the ball of clay with your hands. Using different tools, let the child make impressions in the clay by laying each tool on the clay and moving the rolling pin over it to press down on the tool. Then, lift up the tool to see the results. Also, have children try rolling the tires of the truck through the clay to create tracks. Let children experiment with various tools to see what kinds of "tracks" they can make. Continue the investigation by twisting the screw into a chunk of clay, pinching the clay with pliers, and so on.

Fitting Pipes ✳

Getting Ready: Create an activity set with PVC pipes, joints, and elbows. Use a hacksaw to cut the PVC pipe into different lengths, making several pieces of each length. Start with 4" (10 cm), 6" (15 cm), 12" (30 cm), 18" (46 cm), and 24" (61 cm) lengths. Following the directions on the package, spray the ends with silicone spray so that the pieces can be taken apart more easily. Place the pieces of pipe in a box with several PVC joints and elbows. (All products can be purchased at a home improvement store.)

Activity: Use the pipes and joints to create structures. Let children build pipelines across a table or carpet area. Alternatively, give each child a number and then direct the children to use that number of pipes to build their pipelines. Challenge them to build a short pipeline and a long pipeline using the same number of pipe pieces. When the pipeline is finished, have children roll a small rubber ball through it to see what happens.

Materials

- Box
- Hacksaw
- PVC pipes, joints, and elbows
- Rubber ball
- Silicone spray

Making Medallions & Stepping Stones ✳

When construction workers are building a bridge or a tall building, they must use materials, such as steel girders and concrete, that are strong enough to hold a lot of weight. Concrete is a mixture of sand, gravel, and cement, which is a compound that acts like glue. Concrete is very hard and strong when it dries.

To make medallions, work with two or three children at a time. Give each child a paper cup. Have the child carefully mix together ¹/₂ cup (118 mL) of plaster of paris and ¹/₄ cup (60 mL) of water with a plastic spoon. Discard spoons when finished mixing. *CAUTION: Remind children not to put any of these materials near their mouths and eyes.* Talk about how the mixture is a liquid. Gently press a small toy or token into the plaster. Continue to observe the mixture as it dries. After it begins to set up and before it dries completely, use the end of a paintbrush to drill a small hole through the plaster about ¹/₂" (13 mm) from the edge of the cup. Feel the sides of the cup. It will be warm as the mixture turns from a liquid to a solid. *(Have children thoroughly wash their hands.)* When the plaster has dried completely, discuss with children that the mixture is now a solid. Tear away the paper surrounding the plaster form and string a 24" (61 cm) length of yarn or ribbon through the hole to create a medallion for a necklace.

Alternatively, complete a unique class project by making a stepping stone path. Use real cement product from a home improvement store. Mix as directed *(follow the manufacturer's cautions)* and pour it into disposable foil pans, as many as desired. Wearing rubber gloves, let children decorate the tops of the stepping stones by setting small pebbles into the damp cement. As the cement starts to dry, scratch the child's name on the surface with a stick. Set the pans aside. When the stepping stones are thoroughly dry, remove them from the foil pans and place them on the ground to create a unique path.

Materials

- Cement, small pebbles, and a stick
- Foil pans
- Measuring cup
- Mixing spoons
- Paintbrush
- Paper cups
- Plaster of paris (Read the directions on the package carefully and completely.)
- Plastic spoons
- Rubber gloves
- Small toys or tokens
- Water
- Yarn or ribbon

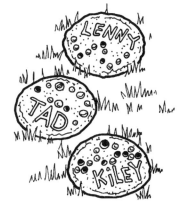

Dump Truck Delivery Math ✳

Materials

- Card stock and marker
- Masking tape or painter's tape
- Small containers filled with manipulatives: pasta wheels, pebbles, small plastic cubes, large blocks, etc.
- Toy dump truck

Getting Ready: On 10 sheets of card stock, draw a large circle and label each one individually with a numeral 1–10. Around a large play area, affix the numbered circles to the floor with masking or painter's tape. In the middle of the room, place several containers of manipulatives.

Activity: Show children the different numbered circles or "work sites" and explain that they need to move the proper amount of construction materials (the manipulatives) to each work site. Let the young "construction workers" choose a work site (reading the number on the circle) and then fill the back of the dump truck with the corresponding number of items. The "truck driver" drives the dump truck to the numbered work site and dumps those items on the corresponding circle. Repeat the activity until the correct load of "building materials" has been delivered to each work site. When children are finished making the 10 deliveries, have them transport all materials back to their original containers—ready for the next work crew!

Traffic Cone Dodging ✳

Materials

- Large cones or poster board and tape or stapler
- Music CD and player

Getting Ready: Obtain a set of large cones or make some by wrapping poster board into a cone shape. Secure the paper cone shape with heavy tape or staples and bend up the paper about 2" (5 cm) from the bottom of the cone to give the cone shape some stability. Place the cones randomly around a large play space.

Activity: Play some lively music and invite children to dodge the cones at your command. The first time around the space have children weave in and out of the cones. The second time, encourage them to jump over the cones. The third time, you might ask them to circle each cone, hop between the cones, walk backward from one cone to the next, or another movement. Continue having children move about the cones and take turns rearranging them for each trip across the play area.

I'm a Fine Construction Worker

(Sing to the tune of "I've Been Working on the Railroad")

Chorus:
I'm a fine construction worker; that's what people say,
I'm a fine construction worker; I like to do this every day.
People come from miles around here to see what's being built.
Don't you hear the foreman shouting? Let's all get to work.

I love to use my hammer, I love to use my hammer,
I love to use my hammer all day long.
I love to use my hammer, I love to use my hammer,
I love to use my hammer now.
(Match the rhythm of the song by pounding your fist on your open palm.)

Repeat Chorus

I love to use my drill, I love to use my drill,
I love to use my drill, all day long.
I love to use my drill, I love to use my drill,
I love to use my drill now.
(Make a rhythmical drilling sound "ZZZZZ" while pointing your index finger and extending your hand forward.)

Repeat Chorus

I love to use my saw, I love to use my saw,
I love to use my saw all day long.
I love to use my saw, I love to use my saw,
I love to use my saw now.
(Make a rhythmical sawing sound "KKKKK" while moving one arm across your other arm.)

Continue by adding other construction tools, movements, and sounds.

Construction Cup Snacks

Materials

- Bowl and mixing spoon
- Chocolate pudding mix
- Chocolate sandwich cookies
- Marshmallows
- Milk
- Small, clear plastic cups
- Small hammer
- Spoons
- Zippered plastic bags

Some construction workers always seem to be working in the mud—the dirtier the better or so it seems! (NOTE: Follow your school's guidelines for serving food in the classroom.) Make chocolate pudding according to the package directions. Place the cookies into zippered plastic bags and crush them by lightly tapping the cookies with a hammer. Have children make construction cups by placing rocks (marshmallows) to form the bottom layer, pouring a layer of mud (chocolate pudding), and then sprinkling some dirt (crushed chocolate cookies) on top. Give each child a shovel (spoon) and dig in. As everyone enjoys the snack, remind children to look for the different layers of rock and soil whenever they pass a construction site where large machines have been digging.

Dramatic Play Center: Construction Zone!

Materials

- Assortment of materials: blocks, rocks, sticks, foam pieces, etc.
- Cone-shaped beverage cups
- Sand table
- Various types of toy trucks for "construction jobs"

Create a construction zone by providing a large sand pile on the school grounds or use the sand table in the classroom. Gather "construction materials," such as blocks, sticks, rocks, rigid polystyrene foam pieces, and so on, for building various structures. If possible, include a few toy construction trucks. Then, young workers can dig in the sand and haul materials on "roads." Decorate beverage cups to look like traffic cones.

Community Connections

Invite one or more of the following people to visit your classroom: carpenter, plumber, electrician, architect, mason or bricklayer, tile layer, painter, carpet layer, etc. Additional information about inviting visitors is provided on page 6.

If possible, plan a walking field trip to a nearby construction site and let children watch (from a safe distance!) how the workers use various machines to get the job done.

Kindergarten Corner: Match the Tool to the Job

Materials

- Assortment of tools
- Paper, pencil, and crayons
- Picture book as listed

Read aloud *Tools* by Taro Miura (Chronicle, 2006) and talk about the different kinds of tools that are used in construction work. Gather an assortment of tools in a toolbox for children to examine and talk about. Be sure to include a few unrelated tools and see if children can identify those that are used for building projects and those that are not. Wrap up the lesson by letting each child trace around a selected tool on a piece of paper and dictate or write a story about using the tool to build something.

File Folder Game: Construction Zone

Materials

- 2 colorful file folders
- Blue card stock (or another color)
- Die
- Index cards
- Markers
- Orange card stock
- Scissors and glue
- Stapler
- Zippered plastic bag

Getting Ready:

1. Make one copy of the "To Play" instruction box on this page and cut it out. Using orange card stock, make 13 copies of the traffic cones on page 152. Write the letters (uppercase and/or lowercase) individually on the cones so that you have at least one of every alphabet letter. Cut out each cone along the dashed lines. Make two copies of the truck cab and bed on page 152. Color as desired and cut out the truck parts.

2. Cut the index cards in half and also write an alphabet letter on each.

3. Cut one of the file folders in half along the fold. Cut the larger panel in half the long way and trim off the tab to make two long strips. On each long strip, glue a truck cab. See the diagram.

4. On the back of the uncut half of file folder, place glue across the top, down along both side edges, and down the middle of the piece. Affix this to the left-hand panel of the second file folder. This will create two large pockets. (The edge along the fold has the openings for the pockets.)

5. Slide the cab strips into the pockets. Glue the beds of the trucks to the file folder so that the front of each bed is aligned with the edge of the pocket and with the cab of the truck. Remove the cab strips from the pockets.

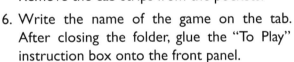

6. Write the name of the game on the tab. After closing the folder, glue the "To Play" instruction box onto the front panel.

7. Laminate the file folder, index cards, traffic cones, and truck cab cards separately. Carefully slit through the lamination along the fold to open up both pockets.

8. Slide the cab card into the pocket so that the only thing showing is the cab. (Trim the edges of the card if necessary). Place the cards, the die, and the cones in a zippered plastic bag and staple it to the back of the file folder.

✂ -

To Play

1. Spread out the cones faceup on the playing area. Stack the cards in a pile facedown.

2. Role the die and pick up the same number of cards as shown.

3. Find the cones that match the letters on the cards. Place the cones on the truck above the dots. If there is not enough room for the cones, pull the truck cab forward to make more space.

4. Play again to load the second truck.

Construction Zone Game
(Refer to directions on page 151.)

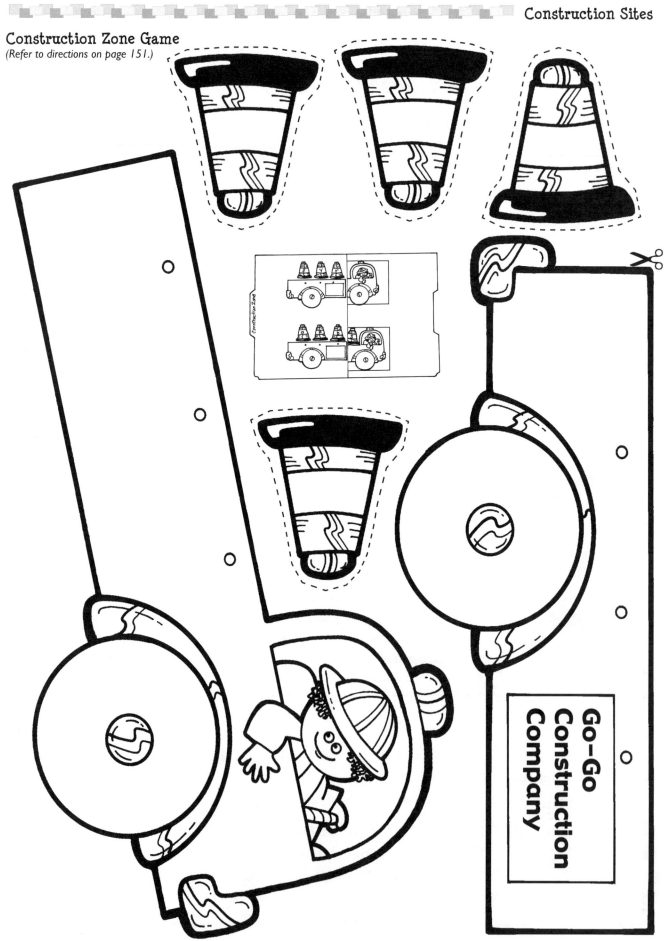

Construction Vehicles *(Refer to directions on page 5 and page 166.)*

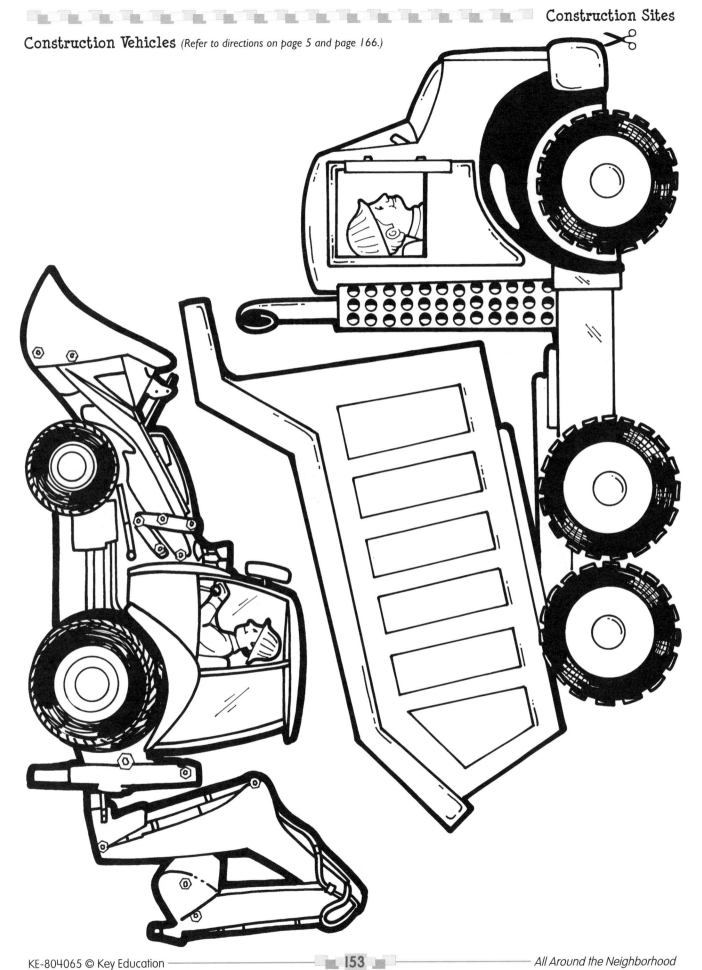

Construction Vehicles *(Refer to directions on page 5 and page 166.)*

ROAD WORK

Restaurants

What Should I Order?

Getting Ready: Make a copy of the booklet on pages 159–162 for each child. Follow the directions on the pattern pages for assembling the booklets.

Activity: Read aloud *Good Enough to Eat: A Kid's Guide to Food and Nutrition* by Lizzy Rockwall (HarperCollins, 1999) or *Gregory the Terrible Eater* by Mitchell Sharmat (Simon & Schuster, 1984) and talk about healthful foods and those that are not.

Show children the food samples you have prepared and have them give you the thumbs-up sign if the food is something that is healthful to eat and a thumbs-down if it is not. Also, talk about foods that are okay to eat occasionally but not every day.

Distribute menus to the class and talk about the healthful choices (if any) that are offered on the menus. Brainstorm with children food choices to order that are good for their bodies.

Give each child a copy of the booklet *What Will You Order?* to complete and color as desired. As indicated on the pattern pages, have the child write the correct alphabet letters in the thought bubbles and fill in the soup bowl.

Materials

- Various foods (some healthful to eat, some not) that can be ordered in a restaurant
- Children's menus (these can be from several different restaurants), one for each pair of children
- Pencils and crayons
- Picture books as listed

On Best Behavior

Begin the activity by directing the class to sit at tables. Ask one child to give each person a plate. Ask other children to pass out knives, forks, spoons, drinking glasses, and napkins. Demonstrate to children how the place setting is created—the plate in the middle, the knife (sharp edge facing the plate) and spoon on the right side of the plate, the fork on the left side of the plate, and the glass above the knife. Have children arrange their own place settings. Tell children that when they eat, good manners include sitting quietly in their seats and placing their napkins in their laps. You may also wish to point out a fun trick. It's a secret signal to the server that tells the server when they are finished with their food and are ready to have their plates taken away. Demonstrate how to put the silverware on a plate at the four o'clock position and then have children practice placing their silverware on their plates.

Read aloud *Froggy Eats Out* by Jonathan London (Viking Juvenile, 2001) and discuss the proper way to act in a restaurant. Hold up the plates you have prepared and talk about each rule and explain why it is important. When you are finished discussing the rules, have children show you with their utensils rather than with words that they are "finished" with the meal. Let children help you pick up the place settings and place them in a box for other restaurant activities.

Materials

- Place setting and napkin for each child
- Paper, pencil, and crayons
- Paper plates to write on
- Picture book as listed

Getting Ready

- Write several rules about good manners and behavior for a restaurant setting, recording each rule on a different paper plate. Include ideas such as stay in your seat, use an indoor voice, don't play with your food, and so on.

Restaurant Aromas

Getting Ready: Gather an assortment of strong spices used in a variety of ethnic dishes. Spices might include cinnamon, curry, poultry seasoning, cloves, garlic, onion, cumin, chili powder, etc. Poke holes in the lids of the small containers using an awl or a hammer and nail. Write a number on each container. Record the same numbers on a piece of paper and make a copy of the numbered sheet for each child. Place a small spoonful of each spice into a separate container. Keep a list of the spices in the numbered containers for yourself.

Activity: Place the prepared containers on a table. (NOTE: Be sure each child is not allergic to any of the spices.) Encourage the child to sort the containers so that they are in numerical order. Have the child sniff the first container and decide whether or not the scent is pleasant. If it is, the child should stick a smiley-faced sticker next to the corresponding number on the numbered paper. Continue sniffing until all spices in containers have been tried. Use the children's papers to graph the class's preferences.

Materials

- Awl or hammer and a nail
- Paper and pencil
- Small plastic containers with lids
- Smiley-faced stickers
- Various spices

"Food-to-Go"

Whenever a person has food left on his plate after a meal at a restaurant, the server may put it in a container for the person to take home. In some restaurants, a server may wrap the food in foil that is formed to look like an animal.

Using sheets of aluminum foil, let children try to wrap plastic play foods in creative ways. Encourage them to create animals or other objects as they wrap the pieces of food. Be sure to reuse the foil multiple times and then recycle it.

Materials

- Aluminum foil
- Plastic play foods

Hurry, Hurry

A restaurant is a busy place. Waiters and waitresses (servers) must hurry to take orders, get the foods, and serve them to customers. Brainstorm with children why it is important to stay in their seats at a restaurant.

Divide the class into small teams. Give each team a box and have the team members stand behind the starting line. Play some lively music, such as the "Flight of the Bumble Bee" by Igor Stravinsky, and have children note the fast tempo. Tell children that they are "servers" in a restaurant and need to hurry to bring the food to the tables. At your signal, the first child from each team takes a tray and *walks* quickly (servers never run in a restaurant) to the table that has the food and dishes. Call out a number and have servers gather the corresponding number of items on their trays and then hurry back to the starting line. If a server drops something on the floor, that child must return it to the table and retrieve a different item. Once each server reaches the team's box and empties the tray, the next child in line walks quickly with the tray to the table. Reverse the game to get everything cleaned up.

Materials

- Plastic play foods
- Plastic or paper dishes and serving containers
- Trays
- Boxes
- Music CD and player
- Masking tape

Getting Ready

- Use masking tape to mark a starting line on the floor.
- Place an assortment of play food and plastic dishes on a table.

Chef Chop-Chop

Materials

- Construction paper for "cutting boards"
- Index cards and markers
- Molding dough
- Plastic knives
- Scissors, stapler, and tape
- White construction paper or commercial sentence-strip paper
- White plastic grocery bags, one for each child

Getting Ready: Write the numerals 1–10 individually on index cards. Laminate a sheet of construction paper to create a "cutting board" for each child. Make a batch of molding dough using your favorite recipe or purchase play clay for the children to use.

To make a chef's hat for each child, cut a sheet of white construction paper into strips or use commercial sentence-strip paper and then staple the strips together to create a headband. Turn a plastic shopping bag inside out so that the printed label on the bag is hidden. Cut 2" (5 cm), including the handles, off the top of the bag. Tape or staple the edges of the bag to the inside of the prepared headband to finish the chef's hat.

Activity: Talk about chefs. A chef is the person who works in the kitchen of a restaurant, cooking the food that the servers bring to the restaurant guests. Early in the day, the chef (or an assistant) spends a lot of time cutting and chopping food so that it is ready to be added to a dish when a certain meal is ordered. That way guests don't have to wait as long for the food. Brainstorm with children a list of other things that a chef may do.

After each child has donned a chef's hat, distribute the paper cutting boards, plastic knives, and balls of molding dough. Let children roll their dough into the shapes of logs. Tell your "chefs" to get their knives ready because you are about to call in an order. For example, hold up the index card with the number 10 on it as you say, "Chef Chop-Chop, I need 10 pieces—right now, please!" Have children cut 10 pieces of molding dough from their rolls. Repeat by ordering another number of cut pieces.

Alternatively, place the numeral cards on the table and have children cut and place the correct number of dough pieces below each card.

Table for Two, Please

Materials

- 2 small tables
- Chairs
- Plastic or paper dishes, cups, utensils, and napkins, enough for seven place settings
- Construction paper for seven place mats
- Menus from a local restaurant

When you go to a restaurant, a host or hostess arranges and sets the table for the number of people in your group. So, if three people are in your group, the restaurant will make sure there is a table with three chairs. If there are six people, they may have to slide two tables together to accommodate everyone.

Have children work in small groups, as restaurant staff, to prepare a table for the number of people they will be serving. Tell children a number from 1 to 6 and have them work together as a team to make sure the table is set with the correct number of chairs, plates, utensils, menus, and napkins. Extend the play by pretending that another person has joined the group late. Ask children to elaborate on what they need to do to prepare the table for this new guest. Another idea: tell the "restaurant-staff team" that one of the children in the group got sick and the child and his parents will not be coming after all. Have them discuss what they would need to do and then remove the appropriate number of place settings. Continue with other scenarios.

While I'm Waiting

(Sing to the tune of "Twinkle, Twinkle, Little Star")

Waiting, waiting, tired of waiting,
Waiting, waiting, for my food,
I sometimes worry I'm not able
To wait until the food gets to my table.
When I'm waiting for my food,
Here is something I can do.
(Perform the suggested action.)

Have each child call out an action that can be done to pass the time when waiting for the food to be served. Suggestions might include twiddling thumbs, drumming fingers, yawning, counting lights on the ceiling, etc. Sing until all children have suggested activities and performed the actions.

Dramatic Play Center: Can-Do Diner

Materials

- Chef's hat and aprons
- Cooking utensils
- Dishes and serving trays
- Dishpan and towels
- Menus, pad of paper, and pencils
- Plastic play foods
- Small tables and chairs
- Tablecloths

Create a cozy restaurant setting in your dramatic play center. Have children cover each table with a cloth and place a centerpiece in the middle of it. Encourage some children to be patrons and others to be workers. Have the servers wear aprons and give the patrons menus, explain the daily specials, take their orders, and serve the food. Other children can act the roles of chefs or workers who clear the tables and wash the dishes.

Community Connections

Invite one or more of the following people to your classroom: restaurant chef, pastry chef, food server, or restaurant manager. Additional information about inviting visitors is provided on page 6. If possible, arrange a field trip to a local restaurant before opening hours for a behind-the-scenes look at what happens there.

Kindergarten Corner: Restaurants of All Sorts

Materials

- Menus
- Picture book as listed

Gather menus from a variety of different kinds of restaurants. Read aloud *Dim Sum for Everyone!* by Grace Lin (Knopf, 2001) or other books about eating foods from different countries. Have children look at the menus and talk about the different and exotic meal selections. (NOTE: Follow school guidelines for serving food in the classroom.) Bring in or invite parents to donate foods from a variety of ethnic restaurants for children to sample.

To the teacher: Make one copy of the booklet (pages 159–162) for each child. Cut out each page along the dashed lines. Collate the booklet pages and staple them together. On page 2, have the child write the letter *d* in the thought bubble.

What Will You Order?

2

"What will you order?" asked server Dee.

To the teacher: On page 3, have the child write the letter *b* in the thought bubble. On page 4, have the child write the letter *p* in the thought bubble.

3

"We have some biscuits spread with honey, made fresh by honey bees."

4

And just fresh from the garden, we have some tasty peas.

To the teacher: On page 5, have the child write the letter *c* in the thought bubble. On page 6, have the child write the letter *t* in the thought bubble.

5

And if you're feeling hungry, we have fish from the high seas.

6

And finally, to drink we have some juice or lemon tea."

To the teacher: On page 8, have the child write a variety of alphabet letters in the soup bowl.

7

I thought it over long, all these choices in my head.

And since I couldn't decide, ...

I ordered alphabet soup instead!

8

Transportation

Materials

- Poster board or chart paper and marker
- Pictures of children on trips

How Did You Travel?

Getting Ready: A few days before this activity, send home a parent note requesting that, if possible, they provide a picture of their child on a vacation or trip. Make a large chart with four columns. At the top of each column, write one of the headings: "Bus," "Subway," "Airplane," and "Car."

Activity: Buses, subways, airplanes, and taxicabs—all can bring us from one neighborhood to another. Have children take turns sharing with the class the photos they have brought from home. As each photo is shown, have the child talk about the neighborhood that was visited while on the trip or vacation. Be sure to ask children questions about what mode of transportation they used to get to their destinations. At the end of the talk, post each picture in the corresponding column on the chart.

Materials

- Craft paper and marker
- Index cards
- Large paper clips
- Picture books as listed
- String or yarn
- Tape
- Zippered plastic bags

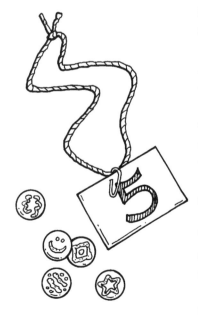

Subway Stops

Getting Ready: Write numerals 1–5 individually on index cards. Also write the same numerals on pieces of paper and tape them to the floor in order around the room to indicate where the subway train stops. String a large paper clip onto a 24" (61 cm) length of string and tie the ends together to make a necklace for each child. Cut circles 1.5" (38 mm) in diameter for subway tokens. Place 10 tokens in a plastic bag for each child.

Activity: The subway is an underground train that moves people from one place to another. Read aloud *Subway Sparrow* by Leyla Torres (Farrar, Strauss and Giroux, 1993), *The Subway Mouse* by Barbara Reid (Scholastic, 2005), or another favorite story about riding a subway train. Encourage children to share about their experiences with using the subway to travel.

Give each child a necklace and a bag of tokens. Have children line up and explain to the class that everyone will need to exchange two tokens for a ticket to ride the subway. As each child pays you two tokens, slip a prepared index card "ticket" into the paperclip on the child's necklace. In their single-file line, have children link together by placing their hands on the shoulders of classmates standing in front of them. Announce in a loud voice, "Welcome to the subway. We hope you have a pleasant ride. We will be stopping at stations 1, 2, 3, 4, and 5 today. Please listen for your stop." Have all children make a shushing noise as they shuffle through the classroom. Lead them around the room to the paper with the numeral 1 on it. Stop the train and announce, "This is station number 1. If your ticket has the number 1 on it, this is your stop. Please exit the train now." Have the children wearing number 1 on their necklace tickets get out of line and sit on the floor near the paper labeled 1. Regroup the subway train car "passengers" and continue the game in the same manner through all the stops until every rider is off the train.

Materials

- An object representing each letter of the alphabet
- Alphabet flash cards (3 sets)
- Juice and small bag of pretzels for each child
- Large block
- Picture books as listed
- Suitcase
- Telephone

Getting Ready

- Tape one set of alphabet cards around the room for places in Alphabet Land.
- Tape a second set of alphabet cards on the floor to represent the airplane seats.

Airplane Ride to Alphabet Land

Airplanes can transport us to faraway neighborhoods. Ask children to help you pack a suitcase because you will be traveling to "Alphabet Land" to visit your alphabet relatives. Explain that you must bring something to give each one of them. Place all of the items you have gathered on the floor or a table. Hold up the letter A flash card and have children identify it. Choose a child to find an object whose name begins with the letter A for your cousin Andy. Place it in your open suitcase. (You may want to put out only a few items at a time, for instance, objects whose names begin with the letters A–G, so that it is easier for children to handle the task.) Continue the activity until something has been packed in the suitcase to represent each letter of the alphabet.

Close your suitcase and pretend to get a phone call. Tell children that you have good news! They are all invited to join you on the flight. Give each child a lettered flash card to use as a ticket and boarding pass and then have children line up to "board" the plane. As they walk through the "security check," use a hand-held "scanner" (wave a large block over their bodies) to look for metal items. Let children find their seats by matching the letters on their tickets to the letters taped on the floor. Collect the tickets after the "passengers" have found their seats.

While children are waiting quietly, encourage them to get comfortable because the airplane will be taking off soon. Tell them to fasten their seat belts and point out where the exits of the plane can be found. Give each child a juice box and a small package of pretzels. (NOTE: Follow your school's guidelines for serving foods in the classroom.) While the plane is "flying," read aloud *Lisa's Airplane Trip* by Anne Gutman (Knopf, 2001), *The Little Airplane* by Lois Lenski (Random House, 2003), *Moon Plane* by Peter McCarty (Henry Holt, 2006), or another favorite title.

When the story is finished, prepare everyone for the landing of the plane and then thank everyone for traveling on [name of airline] flight #321. Tell the passengers that they are now in Alphabet Land. After they get off the plane, have children look around the room for the alphabet flash cards you have already taped in place. Tell them that each letter is the home of one of your relatives and ask them to help you by delivering the things you have packed. Give each child a letter flash card. Have children individually choose the item from the suitcase whose name starts with the letter featured on the card and place it near the same letter flash card that is displayed in the room.

Materials

- Craft or mural paper, construction paper, marker, scissors, and tape
- Pictures of community workers (on pages 17–27)
- Pictures of familiar people, cartoon characters, and animals
- Picture books as listed

Getting Ready

- Draw a large bus on craft paper and display it on a wall or bulletin board.
- Make copies of the community worker pictures and cut them out.

Who's on the Bus?

Buses can give people rides all over the city. Read aloud *Don't Let the Pigeon Drive the Bus* by Mo Willems (Hyperion, 2003), *Next Stop!* by Sarah Ellis (Fitzhenry and Whiteside, 2000), or another fun book about riding the bus. Have children individually select a picture of a community worker. One at a time, ask a child to tape the chosen community worker to the bus you have drawn. As the community worker is added to the bus passengers, sing a new verse of the song "The Wheels on the Bus." For example, sing, "The construction worker on the bus goes pound, pound, pound." Make up a voice and action for each community worker who is riding on the bus.

Extend the fun and play a "Waiting at the Bus Stop" game. Have each child choose a picture from your collection of familiar people, cartoon characters, and animals. Write "bus stop" on a piece of paper and tape it to a chair. Invite three children to come and stand at the front of the room near the bus stop and show their pictures. Ask them to introduce themselves to the class by saying, "Hi, I'm [name of picture]. I'm waiting for the bus." After the three chosen children have introduced themselves, have them turn around to hide their pictures. Ask the children who were listening if they can recall the names of the people in the pictures. Repeat with other children until everyone has had an opportunity to wait for the bus.

Bus Song

Ready for a ride on a bus? Arrange some chairs (one for each child) in two columns with two sets of chairs side by side in each row. Be sure to allow plenty of space between the rows and then let everyone get on board for a fun ride. When the class sings "Our red bus hits a bump," the passengers "bounce" out of their chairs onto the floor and then switch seats with other riders. Everyone will want to sing the song again!

A Bumpy Ride

(Sing to the tune of "Here We Go Looby Loo")

Here we go down the street.

This bus has a schedule to meet.

Our [color word] bus hits a bump,

(Everyone "bounces" onto the floor.)

Bouncing us to a new seat.

Go, Traffic, Go!

Materials

- Black craft paper
- Colorful card stock
- Paper, markers, scissors, and tape
- Pictures of buildings on pages 10–15 and 48
- Pictures of vehicles
- Shoe boxes
- Water bottles and duct or packing tape

Getting Ready: Using colorful card stock, make a copy of the vehicles provided throughout this book. Fill the water bottles with some water to stabilize them and secure the caps with duct tape. Then, cut out and attach each vehicle to a water bottle. Make copies of the buildings on colorful card stock and trim around the pictures as desired. Tape the buildings to the side panels of shoe boxes. Make busy streets around the classroom by taping a black craft paper road on the floor. Include a parking lot in one corner. Place the buildings along the edges of the streets.

Activity: Have children drive and park the vehicles around the classroom neighborhood.

Sort and Count

Materials

- Construction paper
- Egg cartons
- Large zippered plastic bag
- Scissors and markers
- Sets of manipulatives (buttons, pebbles, etc.)

Getting Ready: To make a "bus," cut off most of the lid of an egg carton, leaving a small portion that covers the last two egg cups. The remaining part of the carton's lid serves as the engine hood and cab of the bus and the exposed egg cups are the seats. Decorate the cab by painting it as desired and drawing and cutting out a simple stick figure to be the bus driver at the wheel. In random order, write the numerals 1–10 individually in the bottoms of the exposed cups. Place a large number of buttons or other identical items into the cups for storage. Then, place the bus in a zippered plastic bag. When making additional sets of buses, include different manipulatives for children to use.

Activity: Place the corresponding number of buttons in each egg cup as shown in the bottom of the cup. Let children do the activity again by using another bus and a different kind of manipulatives.

Materials

- Construction paper and marker
- Picture book as listed
- Wagon

Taxi!

Getting Ready: Cut sheets of construction paper in half the long way. Have children make street signs on the strips of paper, using their first names for the names of the roads.

Activity: Show children how to hail a taxi by raising your hand in the air and calling out "Taxi!" Demonstrate how to give directions to the taxi driver so that the driver will know where to take you. Read aloud *The Adventures of Taxi Dog* by Debra and Sal Barracca (Puffin, 2000) or another book about taxicabs.

Direct children to stand around a large play area, each holding a personal street sign. Choose one child to be the "taxi driver." Choose another child to be the "rider." The taxi driver will pull the rider in the wagon. The rider tells the taxi driver, "I would like to go to [another child's name] Street, please." The taxi driver pulls the rider to the child that has been named and lets the rider out of the taxicab. The rider then becomes the taxi driver, and the taxi driver finds a spot to stand with his street sign. A new rider is chosen. Continue playing, making sure that everyone gets an opportunity to be both the rider and taxi driver.

Bus Ride Snack

Getting Ready: Cut a long strip of waxed paper and tape it to the table. Draw a dashed line down the middle of the waxed paper to represent a road. Place the bowls of snack items along the sides of the waxed-paper road. The bowls represent "bus stops" and the snack items are the bus "riders."

Activity: (NOTE: Follow your school's guidelines for serving foods in the classroom.) Have children spread peanut butter (or something else) on their graham crackers. Tell them that the graham cracker is a bus and the peanut butter stands for the seats. They will need to spread the peanut butter all over the cracker so that there is a seat for everyone. Demonstrate how to push the cracker along the waxed-paper road and stop at each bus stop.

Let the child "drive" the bus along the waxed-paper road, stopping several times to allow "passengers" to get on by putting snack items on the cracker. Each child can choose where to stop for more passengers. Finally, have children count the items on their buses before eating the snack.

Materials

- Graham crackers
- Peanut butter or suitable alternative if a child has peanut allergies
- Permanent marker
- Plastic knives
- Small snack items, such as cereal, crackers, and raisins, placed in separate plastic bowls
- Tape
- Waxed paper

Materials

- Card stock in two different colors
- Construction paper
- Lamination material
- Scissors and glue
- Sticky-tack adhesive
- Zippered plastic bag

Fun with Patterns

Getting Ready: Make several copies of page 174 on two different colors of card stock. Cut out each vehicle along the dashed lines. Cut several pieces of construction paper in half the long way. Staple the paper strips end to end to create long work mats. Choose two different vehicles in the same color (two of each kind, four in total) and glue them on the left side of a work mat to create an ABAB pattern. On a second construction-paper work mat, make another ABAB pattern by gluing four vehicles in total, two of each kind in two different colors. Continue making various work mats to provide simple pattern cues for children to use.

Sort the remaining vehicle game pieces into groups by both the color and type of vehicle. Be sure there are enough pieces of each vehicle in the correct color to do each activity. Store each group in a separate zippered plastic bag.

Activity: Demonstrate how to continue a pattern with the vehicle game pieces. For example, an ABAB vehicle pattern might look like the following: blue airplane, yellow taxicab, blue airplane, yellow taxicab, and so on. Using the provided game pieces on a work mat, have the child continue the sequence of the featured pattern. It works well to use sticky-tack adhesive to hold the game pieces in place.

Dramatic Play Center: Children on the Go!

Use any transportation games or ideas listed in this section to set up an airport or a bus, subway, or taxi station. Provide money, tickets, or tokens for riders and hats, steering wheels, and maps for drivers. Chairs, wagons, or riding toys can be used for the vehicles.

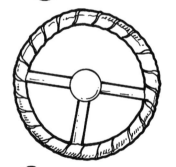

Community Connections

Invite one or more of the following people to visit your classroom: bus driver, taxi driver, subway operator, airplane pilot, flight attendant, and so on. Additional information about inviting visitors is provided on page 6.

Kindergarten Corner: Paying the Bus Fare

Use pennies and nickels to practice paying and getting change for bus fare. Highlight several route cards on city bus maps or make your own routes by drawing paths on a piece of paper. Designate each route as 1¢, 5¢, or 10¢. Have children choose a bus route and then pay the appropriate fare to "get on" the bus.

File Folder Game: On the Move!

Materials

- Colorful file folder
- Hole punch
- Markers, scissors, and glue
- String
- Zippered plastic bag

Getting Ready:

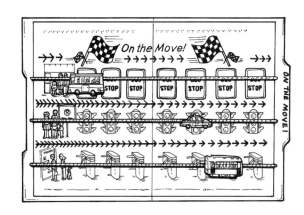

1. Make one copy of this page and the game board on pages 172 and 173. Using card stock, make one copy of the vehicle game pieces and three copies of the cards on page 174. Color all of the game materials as desired. Cut out the "To Play" instruction box, the game cards, and the three small vehicles.

2. Glue the "To Play" instruction box on the front panel of the file folder.

3. Open the folder and orient it so that the tab is on the right. Write the name of the game on the tab. Trim around the game board scene pieces as desired. Glue the two scene pieces to the file folder so that the borders meet at the center of the fold, making three paths for the vehicles.

4. Laminate the folder, the cards, and the vehicles. Trim the pieces as desired.

5. Open the folder and orient it so that the tab is on the right. Punch a hole through the file folder at the left and right ends of each path as shown.

6. Thread a 36" (90 cm) length of durable string through the hole at the left end of the top path. Wrap the string across the back of the folder and pull it through the hole at the right end of that path. Tie the ends in a knot. Then, tape the knot to the back of the city bus game piece.

7. Repeat step 6 with the taxicab (middle path) and subway train (bottom path) game pieces.

8. Store the cards in a zippered plastic bag.

To Play

1. Begin with all three vehicles at the left-hand side of the folder. Place the cards facedown in a stack.

2. Take turns drawing a card and moving the matching vehicle on the game board. Carefully move that vehicle forward one spot by gently pulling on the string.

3. The first vehicle to reach the end of the path is the winner. Count how many stops each vehicle made on the path.

City Bus *(Refer to directions on page 5 and page 166.)*

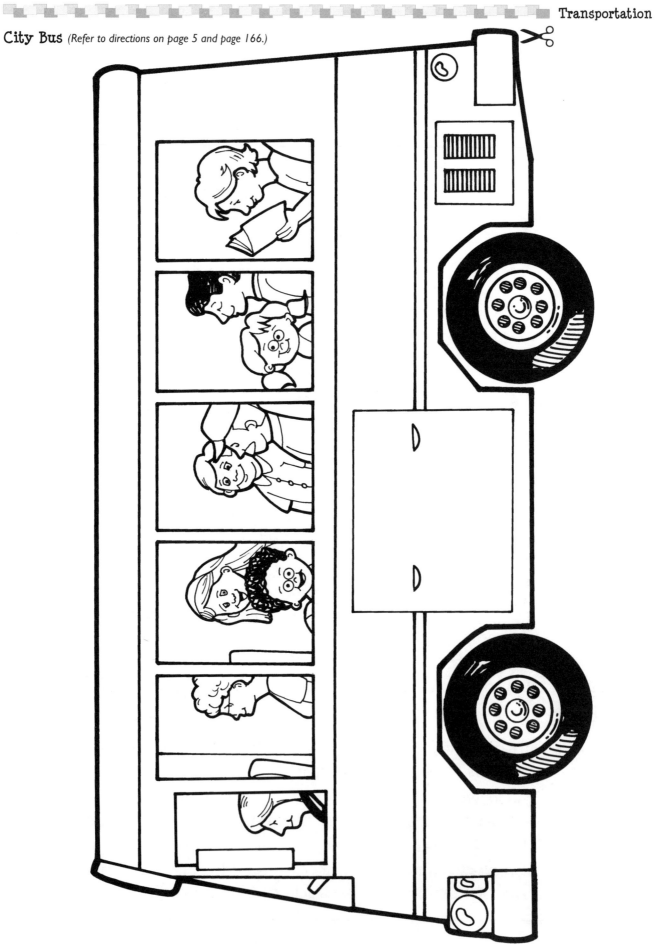

Automobiles *(Refer to directions on page 5 and page 166.)*

171

On the

BUS STOP

BUS STOP

BUS STOP

Taxi Stand

TICKETS

Move!

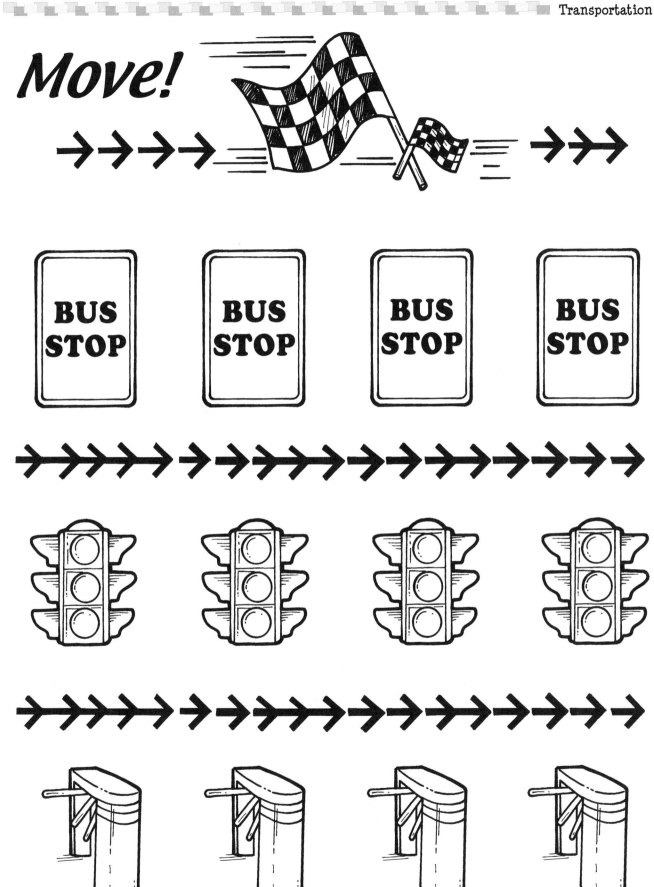

On the Move! Vehicle Game Pieces *(Refer to directions on page 169.)*

Vehicles for Fun with Patterns and On the Move! Game Cards *(Refer to directions on pages 168 and 169.)*

Correlations to NCSS Standards

All Around the Neighborhood supports the National Council of Social Studies (NCSS) *Curriculum Standards for Social Studies.*

The activities in this book support the following performance expectations for students in the early grades:

Culture

1. Students explore and describe similarities and differences in how different groups handle human needs.
The "My Home" section of this book includes an activity in which students learn about different kinds of communities and homes around the world.

2. Students can compare how people from different cultures deal with their environment and their society.
The "My Home," "My School," and "The Library" thematic sections include activities that support this standard.

Time, Continuity, and Change

1. Students can correctly use time vocabulary such as past, present, future, and long ago; read and create simple time lines; identify examples of change; and recognize cause and effect relationships.
There is an activity in the "My Neighborhood" thematic section in which students study the history of their neighborhood and the changes that have taken place there.

2. Students can use various sources, such as documents, maps, textbooks, and photographs to learn about the past.
The Kindergarten Corner activity in the "My Neighborhood" section of this book has students use various sources to learn about the history of their neighborhood.

People, Places, and Environments

1. Students can use maps, globes, and photographs.
Students use a neighborhood map in the "My Neighborhood" section of this book.

2. Students describe how culture, needs, and ideas are reflected in the design of physical environments like homes and classrooms.
The "My Home" thematic section, along with activities in the "My School" and "The Library" sections, supports this standard.

3. Students study how human beings interact with their environment, including land use, the development of cities, and how humans affect ecosystems.
The "My Neighborhood" section supports this standard.

Individual Development and Identity

1. Students can describe personal connections to places, especially those in their immediate surroundings.
Activities in the "My Neighborhood" and "My Home" sections support this standard.

2. Students examine the things that make up their identities, such as their interests and the things they can do.
The *My Book About Me* booklet activity in the "All About Me" section supports this standard.

Production, Distribution, and Consumption

1. Students describe how workers with specific jobs contribute to the production and trade of goods and services.
Each unit in *All Around the Neighborhood* supports this standard through activities, field trips, and classroom visits by various workers.

Correlations to the NAEYC/IRA Position Statement and to NCTE/IRA Standards

All Around the Neighborhood supports the following recommendations for classroom practice from *Learning to Read and Write: Developmentally Appropriate Practices for Young Children*, the joint position statement of the National Association for the Education of Young Children (NAEYC) and the International Reading Association (IRA). This resource also supports the National Council of Teachers of English (NCTE) and the International Reading Association *Standards for the English Language Arts*.

NAEYC/IRA Position Statement

Selected activities in this book support one or more of the following recommended teaching practices for preschool.

1. **Adults create positive relationships with children by talking with them, modeling reading and writing, and building children's interest in reading and writing.**
   The activities in *All Around the Neighborhood* support this standard through classroom discussions, group writing, and read-aloud activities.

2. **Teachers read to children daily. They select high-quality, culturally diverse reading materials.**
   Each unit in *All Around the Neighborhood* includes activities where teachers read high-quality thematic literature to their students.

3. **Teachers provide opportunities for children to discuss what has been read to them, focusing on both language structure and content.**
   All teacher read-aloud lessons in this book are accompanied by classroom discussions.

4. **Teachers provide opportunities for children to participate in literacy play, incorporating both reading and writing.**
   Most units in *All Around the Neighborhood* have dramatic play center ideas that incorporate literacy.

5. **Teachers provide experiences and materials that help children expand their vocabularies.**
   The varied activities in *All Around the Neighborhood* are a great way to expand children's vocabularies in the area of social studies and community helpers.

Selected activities in this book support one or more of the following recommended teaching practices for grades K–3.

1. **Teachers read to children daily and provide opportunities for students to read independently both fiction and nonfiction texts.**
   Each unit in *All Around the Neighborhood* includes activities where teachers read high-quality thematic literature to their students. In addition, this resource book includes many mini-books for students to complete and read.

2. **Teachers provide opportunities for students to write many different kinds of texts for different purposes.**
   In this resource, students write or dictate a wide variety of things, including lists, stories, thank-you notes, and descriptions.

3. **Teachers provide opportunities for children to work in small groups.**
   This book includes many small group activities.

4. **Teachers provide challenging instruction that expands children's knowledge of their world and expands their vocabularies.**
   The varied activities in this book are a great way to expand children's vocabularies in the area of social studies and community helpers.

NCTE/IRA *Standards for the English Language Arts*

1. **Students read many different types of print and nonprint texts for a variety of purposes.**
   In *All Around the Neighborhood*, students read mini-books and texts of various lengths to complete activities.

2. **Students communicate in spoken, written, and visual form, for a variety of purposes and a variety of audiences.**
   During the activities in this book, students communicate orally in class discussions and literacy play, in writing through a variety of group and individual writing activities, and visually in drawing and other art projects.

3. **Students become participating members of a variety of literacy communities.**
   The many group activities and games in *All Around the Neighborhood* help teachers build a literacy community in their classroom.

4. **Students use spoken, written, and visual language for their own purposes.**
   This book provides many opportunities for students to use language independently.